Lifting The Gnostic Veil

Table (

CW01501752

Lifting The Gnostic Veil

Table Of Graphics

Table Of Contents

Lifting The Gnostic Veil

A didactic on the origins of
Paleo-Gnosticism and its influences
on ancient and modern theology

By Malik H Jabbar

Published By

Rare Books Distributor

PO Box 13975

Columbus Ohio 43213

Lifting The Gnostic Veil

Lifting The Gnostic Veil

Library of Congress Catalog Card Number
2007936648

ISBN 10: 1-57154-008-3

ISBN 13: 978-1-57154-008-9

Lifting The Gnostic Veil

Lifting The Gnostic Veil

Finally, we have accomplished what I believe is the definitive book on Religious Mythology. We have explained the "common thread" that is the genitive root of all the world's popular religions, inclusive of Monotheism, Hinduism, Buddhism, and various other religions, some current and some extinguished in history. We have identified certain arcane concepts of Gnosticism that are pervasive throughout all the prominent religious cultures of history, and we have exposed and proven the source from which these ecclesiastical concepts were derived. We have explained *how* and *why* the concepts were generated, and we have proven logically and mathematically the natural genesis, and evolution of these concepts – from the *physics* of nature to the *spirits* of theology.

Within the first section of the book we explain how cultural programming effectively indoctrinates or conditions society, and programs the human psyche to accept and "not resist" (question or investigate) the assertions of illogical and mythical theological concepts. We explain many of the illusions and misconceptions of our cultures, and how these various myths have been intertwined with actual history so as to become indistinguishable. We expound on the inter-workings of culture on the uninformed minds of youth (from toddlers to adults) so as to mold them after any pattern of its cultural choosing – and the difficulties of undoing this mass indoctrination when it has been effectively seeded from infancy into puberty. We explore the cultural creations of the god concept, and the dichotomies of the *conscious soul* and the so-called *immortal soul*, allegedly descended from god and destined to return to god.

We unveil the True Gnosis as opposed to traditional Gnosticism, which is, in fact, another layer of mythological symbolism comparable to that of other mythologically based religions. We trace the origin and development

Lifting The Gnostic Veil

of traditional Gnosticism to its true and lost geneses within the womb of its original formulation, properly described as Paleo-Gnosticism.

We explore the foundations, and sometimes contentious histories of the two tracks of Gnostic symbolism i.e. Monism and Dualism, and correlate same to the controversy concerning the true nature of the mythical Christ, whether or not he was of the same essence as god, or a Prophet imbued with the spirit of god.

In section two, we exemplify the methodology of Paleo-Gnosticism, the ancient esoteric system by which the encrypted language or symbolism of religious mythology is deciphered. Also, incorporating systems of Paleo-Gnosticism, we bring clarity to some of the most cryptic, arcane allegories of the bible. All biblical, and Quranic mythology, as well as Greek, Hindu, and other mythologies are reflective of natural, cultural, or otherwise operable physical phenomena or activities such as astronomy, agriculture, seasonal transitions, and various cyclical events, both natural and cultural. We have correlated the symbolisms with their underlying realities by means of mathematical, graphic, and historical proofs.

In section three, we bring clarity to the mythological symbolism of Jesus Christ, beyond the solar, lunar, and agricultural symbolism that I have already explained, to a significant extent, in my prior writings: *The Biggest Lie Ever Told, 4th Edition*, and *The Astrological Foundation Of The Christ Myth*. The symbolism of Christ in the bible is significantly associated with the Ancient's perception of the origin of the universe, its nature, and functions. We bring clarity to that symbolism.

In the fourth section, we unveil the cycles of actual earthly destructions, or I should say cataclysms and upheavals, as charted by the Ancients. We explain and prove the methods by which the Ancients tracked these drastic alterations in the earth's climate and environment. We prove that the Ancients were obsessed with the tracking of Time for reasons not restricted to seasonal transitions, but for reasons relative to violent and/or tormenting environmental variations that span cycles covering hundreds of thousands of years, and more.

In the last section, or epilogue, I offer some personal observations on the evolution of enlightenment, and the possible structure of future religious society as I see it.

Lifting The Gnostic Veil

Chapter One

The Meaning Of The Gnosis

An Examination Of The Origins And Purposes Of Gnostic
Symbolism

Gnosis Defined

The Gnosis, hidden under the veils of illusion

This world is an illusion, both physically and spiritually. An illusion is
defined as a misconception, a false appearance, an error in perception; a
condition of being deceived by a false perception. Indeed, physically this
world is an illusion, because our perception of reality is not determined by
the *underlying* reality itself but rather by the interpretations that our sensory
organs relay to us of this phenomenal world. We are actually not capable
of perceiving the *ultimate* physical reality with our five senses, because we
are limited by the *interpretive readings* of our senses. Our scientists teach us
that some animals, insects, and fishes do not see the world as we see it
because in some cases their sensory organs are made differently or
calibrated at different frequencies than our own. So what is the *true*
appearance of the world, when it is obvious that if nature or god had
altered or recalibrated our sensory capabilities to different levels and/or
perceptions, the world would appear different without really *being*
different? Is the world we perceive a true representation of what is really
there, or is it an illusion, an interface that transmits signals and
impressions to us in accordance with the calibration and tuning of our
senses - without ever revealing its *true self*? Well, that is an interesting
physics, and philosophical question, but our interest, *at this time*, lies with
the spiritual; with spiritual misconceptions, false perceptions, and illusions.
As noted, we live also in a world of spiritual illusions – but more directly

our *cultural world* is an illusion, inclusive of its religious conceptions, evolved by humanity over countless millennia, which (culture), in fact, is an illusion, a man made illusion. The word illusion also means fantasy, as well as an erroneous and mistaken perception of reality – and this definition of fantasy fits 100% to the mistaken conceptions of the monotheists and others in regards to their cultures, gods, and human destinies. Our goal is to clarify the confusion and misconceptions embodied in our cultural illusions concerning god, history, and human purpose by lifting the veils of mythological symbolism that heretofore have stifled our efforts toward clarity and *right knowledge* concerning religion.

The highways of history, tracking from the distant past to our present era are laden with myths that have been touted as actual truth – these myths carry great symbolism. The Ancients, worldwide, incorporated systems of mythological tales, poems, graphics, orations, dances, festivals, and the like as means of preserving their accumulated knowledge over passing generations. They weaved their histories and scientific knowledge into their various cultural traditions in encrypted form i.e. mythological form, as a means of preserving and restricting vital administrative and instructive data. **But unfortunately these mythologies have come down to us as actual histories rather than as the scientific allegories that they truly are** - pregnant with illuminating symbolism. Also, the means to interpret these encrypted myths have been lost for the most part, so that the ability to interpret these mythological messages is retained by only a select few – and *those,* seers of the hidden wisdom are said to be possessors of the *true* Gnosis.

Our societies, as they stand today, are the culminations of all our known histories embodied in cohesive forms of languages, traditions, behavior patterns, and belief systems. We use the term *culture* to describe this package or accumulation of precepts by which we chart our lives. Our cultures mark the progress or I could say lack of progress in human social

Lifting The Gnostic Veil

evolution to this point in time. Our culture combines or fuses all the evolved traditions, customs, mores, accepted behavior patterns, and belief systems into one *constitution* (whether formally written or not) by which we govern our group (tribe, city, nation, etc). **Our culture is what forms us, molds us into what we are, or think we should be**. The body of traditions, beliefs, and social customs that make up our culture is the mother of our *conscious souls*. I repeat: our culture is the mother i.e. the womb in which our conscious souls gestate and form, so as to become humane or whatever they become.

We humans have all come into this world as blank slates (Tabula Rasa) on which no words were written – the portion of each of our brains that contains our conscious soul was blank, awaiting the impressions of environment, education, and experience to inform it (the conscious soul) of its identity, mission, and direction. We are born without known language, social concepts, religious preferences or political ambitions. **We are birthed from the physical wombs of our biological mothers into the societal womb of our culture**, there to begin and continue a period of social gestation within the confines of our culture or subculture that will mold us, and inform us. Our culture, our created culture, crafted by our own hands (minds) over thousands of years of social evolution, is the womb of our personal human evolution, that makes us what we are or think we are. Its (our culture's) purpose is to create (configure) us socially (as social beings) in the image of itself. And, unfortunately, all of the errors that exist in the mother culture are subject to be duplicated by type in the hearts and minds of its children, and the errors within our cultures are legion – this we will discover as our essay progresses.

We are the products of our cultures, and the flaws (misconceptions) of our cultures have been duplicated in kind in our human psyche, and in some cases highly intensified, depending on our dedication and devotion to the precepts of the culture in whose womb we reside. Our cultures have indoctrinated (programmed) us. In most cases, our birth culture is the only cultural mother that we have ever known or trusted, hence our faith and love in our birth culture is usually absolute and unquestioning. We tend to believe and accept whatever our culture (cultural mother) teaches us, and we do not critically examine or evaluate the dictates of our native cultures as a rule. Our cultures are the cumulative results of thousands of years of social evolution, and our cultures are the embryonic sacs in which our conscious souls (self-awareness) gestate and form. Our cultures are analogous to our biological mother's womb - just as we grew to human physical form (maturity) within the wombs of our mothers, we must also grow to human spiritual and intellectual form (maturity) within the womb of our culture (cultural mother). Our cultures nurture and mold our human psyches, and give birth (awareness and identity) to the conscious soul. As I indicated above, we are born physically without a conscious soul i.e. without known language, moral codes, political or religious preferences, or social traditions except as later inherited from the culture that confines us. Our cultures write (impress) patterns of thoughts upon our brains, and we subsequently, over time, become images of the culture into which we were born.

All gods are born from cultural concepts or I should say *they are* cultural concepts, and these graven idols (images and god concepts) inevitably reflect, at the points of their creations, the stages of intellect, character, ambitions, traditions, hopes, fears, and values of the societies (cultures) that created them - these effete mascots (idols, imagined deities), alleged by their human creators to be divine. All cultures, of course, have religious systems inclusive of god concepts; so consequently, our perceptions of god are normally determined by the societies to which we belong, through systems of cultural programming or indoctrination, by way of our inherited traditions. The *intellectual* quality of a culture is gauged by the accuracy of its rational perceptions while the *inspirational* quality of the culture is gauged by its motivating powers, but the doctrine of a culture need not be genuine (based on truth) in order to inspire, far from it. Inspiration is not rooted in fact but rather in belief, so if the adherents believe their mythological doctrine, it can be a much greater catalyst for their group success than a truth that is not so flattering or appealing.

So our culture is the womb of our temporal conscious soul (psyche), seated upon our enshrouded, innate, immortal soul. Our culture is the fabricator of our outward personalities and opinions, and/or the model by which we design and pattern our social interactions. We judge the quality of other societies by the paradigms accepted as worthy within our own, and most of us assume that our way is the correct way – often to our spiritual detriment, in my opinion. But in truth, our culture is much more than that which I have expressed above – our culture is our controller, our guide, indeed our culture is the mother of our god; and if not for our culture, our gods, as we know (perceive) them, would not exist. **Our gods are concepts, not realities**, but the effects of these false idols are as real as life itself, because of our faith and belief that they (imaginary gods) are real. We attribute our successes or failures to these idols as blessings or punishments from them. Of course the idols neither see, nor speak, nor hear - but we, by way of our expansive imaginations, give them sight, voice, and fantasize that they hear our prayers. We are forever thanking god for blessings that, in truth, we bestowed upon ourselves; or praying for relief from perceived punishments that are actually the consequences of our own stumbles or random adversities.

We are the creators of our culture – it has evolved *through us* over thousands of years of social evolution. **When any culture reaches maturity**, as ours has, it develops a life of its own; in fact it (the culture) develops a mind of its own – and we are ruled by that mind. Our culture represents our *collective mind*, that is to say the aggregate minds of all of us in this generation and, perhaps more significantly, the minds of all those that came before us, down through the centuries, that contributed their minds (thoughts and ideas) to the establishment of our culture. Our *god concept* has been born out of this collective mind, influenced by our environment and experiences over the centuries. The edicts of our gods, their theologies are written in our cultures, so that actually god and culture cannot be separated – hence we sometimes describe our cultures as Judaic, Christian, Moslem, or with some other pertinent religious connotation. Our gods represent our cultures, including the flaws within our ideologies, just as the pagan gods of old represented their various cultures. When the Ancients worshipped the Golden Calf, Dagon, Baal, or some graven image of whatever type – that image was representative of a theology, a culture, a belief system that was thereby personified in a given physical, idolatrous form. The same holds true for our modern idols: Yahweh, Jesus, and Allah - they are personifications of their separate cultures, in the same or similar way that a sport team mascot is the image (personification) of the team. I don't mean to be disrespectful of religious people by referring to their gods as mascots, but I want to force home a point that is highly important to explaining the correct relationship between god and culture. Just as the team mascots would not exist save for the team, our imitative (false) gods would not exist save for the cultures that spawned them. The effect of this reasoning which I wish to convey, which is so important to the elucidations of certain matters that we shall shortly cover, is that the **collective mind embodied in our created culture is the actual spirit (intangible) god that we serve and obey**, a type of incarnation of our religious theories that have developed over the centuries. The popular images of our faiths that we revere so highly, do not exist literally, and are all myths, but as esoteric symbols they are very real illustrations of potent underlying truths - and the creator of all is the collective mind of mankind. The *collective mind* is the only spirit (intangible) god, for good or bad, that can be *intellectually verified*, by tracing its cultural genesis and evolution; and this mind of god (gods) is embodied in the various cultures that profess such beliefs, and is personified in assorted graven idols, images, and/or concepts. This is not to say that a *true* god[1] does not exist - the existence of an incomprehensible god is definitely implied, implied by nature itself – it (nature) screams of intelligent design, but we are not capable of comprehending the nature of the creator god *that preceded time and matter*, according to the Ancients.

Structure of mythology

The word *Gnosis* means knowledge i.e. hidden knowledge or enlightenment; and knowledge, that is to say *right knowledge* is our salvation according to the scriptures. The true Gnosis is a special knowledge, an arcane and obscure perception that interprets what lies beyond the veil of the apparent realities of this world. **Mythology is the mother of *true* Gnosticism.** If not for mythology or I should say if not for the encrypted language of mythology, there would be no Gnosticism (hidden knowledge) because the need would not exist. Mythology was the encrypted language of the Ancients, the system by which they recorded and preserved their agricultural, institutional, traditional, cultural, and scientific data over time. The first forms of mythology were oral, poetic verses and stories that were easy to remember and pass from generation to generation as tribal traditions. These orations conveyed symbolic messages; encoded cultural, astronomical, agricultural, and other vital information that tracked the intellectual advancements of their societies, and were primarily decipherable by the sacerdotal classes and the royalty. We must remember that initially the Ancients did not have libraries or great monuments in which to stow or draw or write their histories or records; but nevertheless, each generation's advancements, records, and history had to be carried forward in some form that could be referenced by succeeding generations – and the form of choice with few other options, if any, was oral traditions i.e. allegorical anecdotes and fables.

---

[1] I define "true god" as the Creator god, the First Cause i.e. the pre-existent state or condition that generated the phenomenal world

Lifting The Gnostic Veil

The mission of true Gnosticism anciently was to decipher these fables, translate the encrypted language to the common vernacular, for the use of the leadership, so that society could benefit and learn from the efforts and accomplishments of the preceding generations, and, more importantly, prepare for the cyclical environmental problems of the future. Mythology is, in truth, a packaging, a type of sealed envelope or locked box, if you will – a vaulted container fashioned for securing, concealing, and transferring information forward to succeeding generations.

Mythological stories are undeniably absurd to any rational mind – they speak of multi-headed monsters, talking animals, and fantastic feats of magic that cannot possibly be true, that is to say literally true; however many religious people accept these tales as actual facts and authentic history, as a matter of faith. For instance, they believe that someone named Moses parted the Red Sea with a shouted command and a magic wand (rod); that someone named Jonah lived inside a fish for three days; that someone named Samson was able to displace the roof supports of a massive building so large that it contained at least 3,000 people, according to the bible, with the push and shove of his mighty arms; that someone named Joshua sent a request to god to stop the sun and moon in their courses, and the request was granted; that someone named Jesus, and Muhammad also in his time, flew through the skies like mythical flying creatures[2], and so forth and so on.

Most of humanity, the common people, are superstitious and gullible, and don't think things through, as a rule. They are concerned mainly with creature comforts – not the *hows* or *whys* of anything, just the results and the effects on their needs and desires. They possess little spiritual initiative (lots of faith but not much healthy skepticism), and tend to follow the paths in life most traveled (crowded) by others, with little thought of why

---

[2] The bible claims that Jesus flew through the skies to heaven, and the Quran claims the same for Muhammad .

– they generally judge truth or error by popular consensus, and not by thoughtful evaluations of pertinent facts. Once society sets a course for them, they tend to stay that general course with little deviation, unless environment and circumstances change so drastically that they are forced to re-think their opinions or, more probably, look elsewhere for guidance. Popular lies (myths) and oft-repeated lies (myths), no matter how absurd, tend to be acceptable and believable by the masses, especially when religious faith is part of the equation. This is the attitude of the proletariat of today, and this same attitude prevailed among the commoners of ancient times. According to some: normally about 85% of any given population fits into the category I have just described – and the remaining 15%, to which you and I belong, tends to be of a more discerning character. So the *irrationality* of most people who blindly follow nonsensical religious dogma is not knew, but rather is consistent with recorded history. Be that as it may, intelligence is the natural enemy of ignorance, and consistent with the prodigious advancements of science in recent centuries, many of yesteryears religious fallacies have become almost impossible for even the most devoted adherents to accept as literally true.

But regardless, the purpose of the true Gnosis is *not* to dissuade people of their cherished beliefs (an almost impossible task when the indoctrination is deep seated after several years of social programming) but rather to bring greater clarity to their beliefs by opening up the illuminating windows of verifiable facts, logic, and reason. True Gnostics support the right of the general populace to follow whatever religious doctrine they may choose at the exoteric level. However, historically they have worked assiduously to influence the structure of various religious doctrines so that the underlying interpretations were not corrupted by *incorrect* symbolizations – because all ancient religion (mythology), at its core, was symbolic. This was the case in the time of the early Christians, when the Gnostics (of which some were enlightened, and others traditional (literal believers)) appeared among them and engaged in fierce philosophical battle with the novices among the early Christians, to prevent them from perverting the *exoteric* symbols of religious dogma by which the *esoteric* meanings are discerned. **Let me interject at this point** that Gnostics are not of one mind; there are differences of outlook and emphasis among the Gnostics just as there is among other societies. Furthermore, in regards to the esoteric knowledge of discernment i.e. the ability to correctly interpret encrypted mythology – this ability has not been manifested, so far, by those who practice Gnosticism as a religion, or philosophy; and take the Gnostic doctrine as literally true. In fact, traditional Gnosticism is, itself, mythology. The traditional Gnosticism of the past and the present – though it possesses valuable insights - is not the source for the correct understanding of the esoteric wisdom, it is simply another belief or faith (a number of faiths really). Their beliefs are just as mythological as Monotheism, Buddhism, Hinduism, and all the rest. Their teachings do not interpret the true Gnosis nor is it *the* Gnosis itself, it is simply another layer of symbolism, to a great extent. We shall bring clarity to the Gnostic symbolism within this book.

I should add at this point that there are different levels of Gnostic understanding – some Gnostics interpret at a mystical level that is more of a delusion than truth. They have knowledge, and some insight, but they have unknowingly perverted it so that it is not much different than the religious mythology that it claims to interpret, or rise above. Actually they have interpreted or expanded the religious symbolism with another layer of Gnostic symbolism that is just as confusing as the former, and requires its adherents to *use more faith than logic* in their pursuit of the salvation that Gnostic wisdom is supposed to bring. **This form of traditional Gnosticism is <u>not the original</u> Gnosticism that was used by the enlightened of old.** We shall explore, in due course, the original Gnostic wisdom - concepts firmly based on the facts of nature and physics, hence a true (correct) wisdom that requires not so much faith as scientific deductions and rational reasoning. The key to higher Gnostic discernment is to remember the trademark phrase that I have repeatedly noted in most of my books: *Spirits based on Physics* – this is the basis upon which the Ancients established the true (correct) Gnosticism.

From this point forward we shall adjust our terminology so as to distinguish between *Traditional Gnosticism* and the ageless Gnosticism of the Ancients that was fashioned hand and glove with mythology as a means of correctly interpreting the encrypted language of mythology. We shall refer to the Gnosticism that represents the ability to interpret esoteric symbolism as *Paleo-Gnosticism, or Paleo-Gnostics*. The Gnosticism that I have used in my other books to bring clarity to certain arcane scriptural symbolisms, and will use also within this book shall henceforth be termed *Paleo-Gnosticism, or Paleo-Gnostics* – this terminology should alleviate any possible confusion that otherwise might ensue. **Paleo-Gnosticism is the original system used by the Ancients to interpret mythology** – it is important to understand that it is not a philosophy, and definitely not a religion, but rather is a scientific methodology. As noted above, ancient mythology was the means by which the Ancients recorded their cultural and scientific data, in encrypted form. The mythology over the millennia became ecclesiastical, and subsequently or perhaps concurrently, within a religious context, was recorded as historical instead of mythical. It is through the use of scientific methods of deduction, incorporating the systems of Paleo-Gnosticism that we are able to cut through the mire of cultural traditions and religious illusions and thereby ascertain correct understandings of the mythological symbolisms. The true Gnosis i.e. Paleo-Gnosticism is the *link* between the exoteric and the esoteric; Paleo-Gnosticism unveils the masque of religious mythology by rendering *intellectual* interpretations of the underlying realities upon which the mythologies are based. The underlying realities may be cosmic, agricultural, cultural, or environmental, and are almost always related in some way to the correct tracking of time, from cycles of twenty-four hours on to cycles that cover millions of years – all this we shall prove as we continue forward.

I should mention also that the mythical Jesus is a profound Gnostic symbol, and his life as portrayed in the bible is of immense Paleo-Gnostic import; not only in reference to the solar and lunar symbolism, but far beyond that - to the structure of the macrocosmic universe as they anciently perceived it, and the relationship of mankind (the microcosm) to this grand universe. Fortunately, the Gnostics were successful in imbedding their Gnostic symbolisms into the Christian scriptures - detailed explanations of this are offered further on in the book.

Dynamics of Paleo-Gnosticism

As I noted above, mythology is metaphorically a locked container by which vital data was transported by the Ancients from generation to generation over thousands of years. **Paleo-Gnosticism is the key** that unlocks the mysteries of mythology, and opens the path that leads to correct understanding of the *esoteric* wisdom - veiled by the *exoteric* masque of mythology. Traditionally speaking, Paleo-Gnosticism is not a religion, but rather it is a form of enlightenment – it is the insight (derived primarily through scientific study) to perceive hidden meanings within various forms of symbolisms, such as cultural, agricultural, cosmic, architectural, scriptural writings, and more. Actually as we proceed further into our investigations of the *traditional* Gnosis, I will introduce concepts that veer from the conventionally accepted conceptions of traditional Gnosticism, and I will bring forth proofs of the underlying reality upon which traditional Gnosticism is based and was founded; but first we need to explore the traditional concepts thoroughly because some of the arcane and puzzling Hebrew mythological tales that we shall soon interpret, relevant to spirituality or the journey of the soul, are based on traditional Gnostic concepts.

The Meaning Of The Gnosis

Lifting The Gnostic Veil

Paleo-Gnostics do not have exclusive scriptures of their own, that is to say hidden scriptures that contain clear explanations of esotericism in common (non-symbolic) language. They use the same scriptures that the sacerdotal classes use or have access to, but their interpretations of these scriptures goes beyond the common pale. Paleo-Gnostics are visionaries that see beyond the pale, but outwardly they may be Christians, Muslims, Jews, Buddhist, Hindus, Atheists, Agnostics or whatever. They may even be mercenaries or criminals! We may also find Paleo-Gnostics among our politicians, ministers, soldiers, actors, athletes et al. We must understand that Paleo-Gnosticism is a *rational* enlightenment that feeds the intellectual soul – it (Paleo-Gnosticism) is not mystical but rather spurs mental clarity as pertains to the true character of god – and our situation on this planet, which Plato and some others in history likened to hell. The effect of this knowledge on *some* personalities is that it brings the worst of human nature to the fore, so that they lose their humanness and are almost totally devoid of compassion and empathy - they tend to become merciless predators and deceivers of the human populace, and look upon the masses as fodder for their economic and sensual appetites. Paleo-Gnostics are identified by what they *know*, not by what they outwardly profess, and certainly not by character. Have no doubt, that among the Rabbis, Ministers, Imams, politicians, evangelists, spiritualists, monks, teachers, and others that shout religious, philosophical, political, and social lies and fantasies to their flocks on a regular basis, there are those that possess some degrees of the esoteric wisdom; however they find it to their advantage to conceal the esoteric wisdom or use it for their personal and/or group advancement. Many of them believe that the masses are not capable of handling the real truth; and they may be right – in fact, I'm sure that they are right in that respect, based on the history of how the Ancients concealed the truth from all but those that proved their worth through systems of strenuous initiations. But nevertheless, I believe that we can successfully move the general society to a higher awareness, and in reality we must do so, because monotheism has run its course and it's only a matter of time before it dies a natural death – because monotheism cannot withstand the scrutiny of intelligent minds that have not been previously blinded by faith. Most monotheists, I believe, are nominal believers not dedicated believers, and certainly not zealots; and as intelligence and awareness among the populace grows with each succeeding generation, monotheism will certainly wail and regress.

So if I may reiterate, Paleo-Gnosticism, as defined in this book, is not a faith or system of religious beliefs or tenets, but rather **Paleo-Gnosticism is a scientific methodology** by which we are able to correctly interpret or translate religious and spiritual mythology. Paleo-Gnosticism is the interpretive link between the obscure symbolisms of mythology and the underlying veiled realities that the mythology represents. **This definition is not the conventional meaning of the term *Gnosticism*,** but it was the original meaning when used by the Ancients, that described a secret *scientific knowledge* that was not shared with the general public. *True* Gnosticism i.e. Paleo-Gnosticism is *not* a secret *spiritual knowledge* as we have been misled to believe. However, higher spirituality for *some* may result from increased scientific understanding of the *patterns* of nature, the symbiotic interactions of matter and spirit, and the cycles of time – we shall elucidate on this further on in our essay. Traditional Gnosticism, we must say, is actually another form of symbolism, similar to astronomical mythology, and actually the child of some forms of astronomical mythology, that was written to symbolize ancient man's mistaken conceptions of the universe's configuration. **A major goal of this book is to prove the cosmic genesis of traditional Gnosticism,** that is to prove that traditional Gnosticism was born of mankind's misconceptions of certain astronomical structures - and to unveil and explain the meaning and purposes of the true Gnosis i.e. Paleo-Gnosticism, consistent with our most recent definition of the term.

It is widely accepted that the ancient Gnostics alleged that they possessed a secret knowledge, unknown to the common masses, and that this knowledge was key to salvation. This was true originally but has not been generally true of those that advocate this doctrine, not for thousands of years. The term Gnostic has evolved to refer to people that share similar philosophical beliefs concerning god, nature, and man – but these Gnostic beliefs are not unique overall, and certainly not secret. The Gnostics, as a group or groups, lost the secret knowledge many years ago. **That which I refer to as Paleo-Gnosticism *is* the secret knowledge,** that is to say the secret knowledge of how to decode religious allegory. It (the secret knowledge) is the knowledge of the methodology that links the symbolisms of religious mythology with the underlying realities that they allegorically represent. And in regards to the secret knowledge leading to salvation – it did not originally refer to spiritual salvation per se, but rather to *intellectual salvation* – salvation *for the rational mind* lost in confusion and bewilderment concerning our place (function) in this universe, and our ultimate destiny. Let me reiterate, *intellectual salvation will lead inevitably to spiritual salvation,* because through unveiling the secrets of physical nature, we are brought into intimate relationship with the intelligent designer, its thinking, its methods; but the salvation that the Gnostics and other religionists of all stripes seek is an illusion – an illusion that follows a myth, religious myth. Religious myth requires faith to support its claim to salvation but faith alone does not bring solace to the logical and inquisitive rational mind. **The rational mind has been designed by nature (or god if you like) to absorb and evaluate facts**, in order that we might successfully interact with our environment; and any genuine salvation must eventually satisfy the hunger of the rational mind for facts, or for formulas that promise a means by which to divulge facts; otherwise our minds will be steeped in confusion – as many are. Our brains (minds) are the instruments that we must use to successfully find truth – not faith, trust, and hope; and our brains have been designed to interact, to network within the confines of the natural order i.e. the confines of time and matter. The brain cannot function outside of the limits for which it was designed. Although the brain can imagine anything – it needs facts, or a

The Meaning Of The Gnosis

belief in presumed facts, before it can derive valid, or sometimes through error, invalid conclusions; and of course, mistaken facts lead to false conclusions. The Ancients concluded that God (the first cause) was unknowable, and I, for what it's worth, concur wholeheartedly, because our brains cannot coherently calculate *timelessness* or *disembodied intelligence*, which is the alleged composition of God. Our brains need sequence (time) and substance (matter) in order to function (compute) properly. Let me interject here – my experience has been that if we view the entire universe as mechanical and everything within it as mechanical (automatous), including ourselves, this will help us in the discovery of real truth, be it pleasant or unpleasant. It must be remembered: freewill and imagination, those complimentary offspring of human intellect are the traits that make us superior to all other animals. All other creatures are slaves to instinct, automatons that cannot see (imagine) things beyond their environment or physical senses.

All religions claim that ultimate salvation is reunification with god, that we have souls which are housed in our bodies, that yearn for their eventual returns to god - hence salvation; and furthermore that unity with god does not come in this life but in the hereafter, a hereafter that is ethereal, spiritual – so it seems to me that we are defeated before we start, that is in terms of solace for the rational mind – because our minds are *not* designed to evaluate systems, such as an immaterial spiritual heaven, that lay outside of the bounds of time and matter. Our brains cannot compute issues that lay outside of the governance of the physical world, that are not bound by the natural laws that our brains are designed to interact with. This type of spiritual salvation requires faith to sustain it as a belief system - it is not compatible with factual analysis. We are required, if we follow the various dogmas that vie against reason, to have faith that our beliefs are true, and will really lead to reunification of our souls with god. Actually, salvation does not sound very appealing to me, that is to say reunification with god in heaven – I love my freedom too much. I can't imagine living for an eternity under the oppressive guidelines that I imagine must prevail in heaven - however to each his own. But back to the point – **true salvation is when we learn our function, destiny and relationship with nature,** thereby alleviating the confusion, fear and doubt that accompanies the ignorance of same. Salvation is not a place or destiny, or an end point - but rather a state of mind (rational mind), a system of paradigms that satisfies the rational mind's lust for logic. Of course our *emotional* and *passionate* minds may *team up* and overrule the reasoning restraints of our rational minds, and produce the *illusion of salvation* by means of any doctrinal path that we may choose to follow, and trust by faith – but that will not work for those of us in whom the rational mind is the dominant character.

As I have indicated previously, Gnosticism is sectionalized as are all religions, but there are certain tenets of the Gnostic creed that are traditional to all Gnostics regardless of their denominations or affiliations; and these basic tenets are also traditional within various religions that have been influenced by Gnosticism, of which there are many. All religions have aspects of Gnostic belief within them or hold certain Gnostic precepts in common, whether openly identified as such or not. **There is a common thread that runs through all religions** that is of Gnostic origin i.e. a trend of thought that parallels Gnostic precepts, and therefore indicates a certain commonality of religious attitude going far back into prehistory. A major purpose of this book is to unveil that common thread, *prove its astronomically based origin*, and thereby concurrently prove that Gnostic belief is simply another form of mythological symbolism. In regards to this commonality that exist among all religions i.e. this common thread of precepts that we are labeling as Gnostic – we should not get hung up on the term Gnostic as a means of identifying this commonality, but rather we must focus on the dogma itself that represents this oneness of spiritual thought.

Lifting The Gnostic Veil

Now, let us review some of the basic tenets of traditional gnosticism, as believed by those who identify themselves as Gnostic, and also others of various religious persuasions, ancient and modern, that incorporate within their dogmas aspects of traditional Gnostic beliefs. There is actually a withering array of varied so-called Gnostic concepts, but the following tend to be basic to the creed. Our aim is *not* to cover all popular Gnostic precepts, but only those that are in focus with our objective of proving the mythological origin of traditional Gnosticism.

Gnostic Overview:

God: Basic to Gnosticism is the belief that god is transcendental spirit, that god, the first Cause, is unknowable. God is limitless, immaterial, and eternal according to Gnostic doctrine. God is the source of all, he is the unbegotten Father, unchanging, perfect, incomprehensible, invisible spirit, indefinable, ineffable, and has always existed.

Cosmogony: There are two popular trends of belief, versions, or views on the origin of the universe, among Gnostics; one being pantheistic in focus, and the other view may be considered as dualistic, though both versions tend to blend and overlap. The pantheistic view propounds that the universe is the result of emanations from the divine source i.e. the unknowable god. God created the universe, or it is better to say, that god caused the creation of the universe through a series of emanations – each emanation in turn produces a lesser emanation, that is, of course, more distant from the divine core (god) than the former, and therefore less endowed with the sacred qualities of the central source of all i.e. god. Each succeeding emanation, as it expands outward from the divine source, is said to become increasingly engrossed in matter, and matter is alleged to be antithetical to the nature of the sacred god source. God is completely devoid of matter, in that god is pure righteous spirit. Gnostics look upon matter as a deterioration of the spirit, a corruption of the spirit, and the opponent of the spirit. The last stage or lowest phase of the emanations is man, or, I should say the universe of man, this visible, physical world, the cosmos, the macrocosm - of which man is the microcosm, according to their (Gnostic) interpretation. Each emanation, according to the Gnostics, represents or is an aspect of god, an Aeon, a spiritual sphere, an Archon, and forms a series of spiritual planes (the Seven Heavens). These seven heavens, or planes, or steps chart the return path that the human soul must pass in pursuit of spiritual salvation, once it is released from the human body. This series of emanations, the totality of all, forms the heavenly Pleroma, the spiritual highway and bridges that the human soul must successfully traverse in search of ultimate salvation, which is reunion with god. A very important version of Emanationism was penned by Plato: according to Plato, the universe was made material and visible by the outflowing of god's will, his emanating spirit. In other words the invisible, nonmaterial form, or idea of the universe existed in the mind of god as thought, intelligence, wisdom, as a spiritual archetype we might say or a seed that subsequently germinated, and became real or material by the creative power of god's will. Plato's version of Gnostic Emanationism is very significant, potent, and impressively symbolized within Christian doctrine, which we shall analyze as we proceed, in due course. It is clear that according to Gnosticism, the universe, the world of matter was begotten (emanated) by god through direct emanation or through series of emanations that are traceable to the unseen god as the original generating force.

The dualistic version of creation relates the birth or development of a lesser god, an opposing god, an imposter that is however the true creator of the physical world. This god came about as the result of an error in the forces of emanation according to some Gnostics, or as the result of the impertinence of associate Aeons (emanations). However developed, whether by error or by impertinence, the world of matter i.e. the physical universe is considered the adversary of the unknowable spiritual god. This lesser god, sometimes regarded as evil and sometimes not, depending on the text, is called by some the Demiurge, or Yaldabaoth, or Ialdabaoth, and by various other names, depending on the language and culture of the adherents to the various Gnostic versions. Some say that the god of the Old Testament was actually the Demiurge, and that the competition, so to speak, between the redeeming faith of Christianity and the oppressive tyrannical law of Judaism is the battle, perhaps final, between the good god of faith and the evil god of oppression (Judaic law)[3]. The Demiurge is the Lord of matter, and holds captive within matter the divine spark or light of the unseen spiritual god, or in some versions the spark of god is resident in matter by divine plan as a source to which our captive souls can link to reconnect with the true spiritual god and eventually overcome and destroy the evil world of matter, along with its deity, Yaldabaoth. However or whatever, all Gnostics agree that we, mankind, are essentially spiritual beings, that are now held captive in matter – that we (our immortal souls) formerly existed as spiritual beings devoid of corrupting matter, and the effects of corruptive matter - within the domain of the spiritual god. But we have landed into the clutches of Satan, the god of matter, and in turn have been enslaved by Satan (matter) and this condition of enslavement of our immortal souls to matter is tantamount to death (of the spirit, soul). Salvation or resurrection of the spirit is when we successfully escape from the bondage of Satan (matter) and return to our spiritual origins – with god.

Salvation: According to Gnosticism, salvation is the reunification of the soul with god. Gnostics believe that we have fallen, stumbled, or have otherwise been exiled from our prior spiritual states into the prisons of matter (our carnal bodies). They believe that what we call life is really

---

[3] There is, indeed, a political/religious view among some Christians and Muslims that Jews are the instruments of Satan.; they are dedicated to the eradication of the so-called Jewish menace. This exemplifies the innate horror within monotheism when adherents believe that their political attitudes have the sanctions of their gods, and they consequently pursue pernicious agendas based on this erroneous assumptions. Most of the world's conflicts are traceable to variances between the monotheists.

death, death of the spirit or enslavement of the spirit within our human bodies. They hold that the pathway to resurrection or freedom is the secret knowledge of how to evoke certain hidden spiritual forces that will enable us (our souls) to escape from the captive forces of Satan (matter). We are presently enslaved to matter, and the struggle between good and evil is actually the struggle of the spirit to escape from its bondage to matter – matter is inherently evil. This struggle of the captive spirit is manifested in various Gnostic and associated traditions or customs; such as Fasting, Asceticism, Celibacy, Meditation, Prayer, emasculation, and abstention from all or various forms of sensual pleasure. The fundamental goal of these religious rituals is to weaken the hold of evil matter i.e. the human body upon the imprisoned soul, in accordance with Gnostic doctrine. The rationale behind this is that all sensual pleasure strengthens matter, and enhances the powers of matter over the imprisoned souls - so by denying the body the pleasures of the senses we better enable the soul in its struggle to eventually escape from its bondage to Satan (matter) - or we help to strengthen the soul so that it does not succumb to the wiles and temptations of the physical body, and thereby disqualify itself for eventual redemption. The Gnostics believe that ultimately a savior will come, or that Jesus was the savior that came from the Pleroma with the mission of enlightening humanity with the secret knowledge of redemption that will free our souls and the captive or resident spark (of god) within matter, and thereby usher in the final destruction of Satan (matter) and lead to our final salvation, that is to say reunion with god in heaven or its equivalent.

The above, in a nutshell, explains the basic tenets of Gnosticism. In truth, Gnosticism, as described above, and by whatever name we may choose to designate it, is the root, the core, the religious, philosophical foundation on which all religions have been formulated – ancient and modern. Let me repeat: All of the world's religions, inclusive not only of monotheism, but also Buddhism, Hinduism, and the countless dead religions that have

The Meaning Of The Gnosis

Lifting The Gnostic Veil

expired over the millennia - *all are derived from a common pattern of beliefs*, suitably described as Gnostic or by whatever label we may choose to identify that belief system. The tenets expressed in the religious creeds of those that we currently classify as Gnostics are remnants of that lost source or system. Even if the doctrines have been diluted and modified, which always happens over time, the core values (basic opinions and viewpoints) remain the same.

Let us reiterate the basic fundamentals of Gnosticism, and compare them to other religious doctrines in general, so as to clarify my assertion that Gnosticism or Gnostic religious philosophy, however labeled, is the tree to which all other branches of religion are seminally connected. **Note, as similarly numerated above**, that Gnostics believe that god is # 1: pure omnipresent spirit and intelligence not limited or contained within physical boundaries; that # 2: god is the source and force of universal creation; that # 3: humans are spiritual beings or immortal souls disjointed from our spiritual roots, temporarily inhabiting mortal bodies that do not represent the true substances of our spiritual nature; and # 4: salvation is defined as successful reunification of our immortal souls with god. I submit that all religions share these identical core beliefs in common, somewhat modified within their separate religious cultures.

First off, to reinforce my point - **all religions represent god as spirit**, whether as a personal god or as a universal soul, the basic context is identical – incorporeal spirit. All religions assert, in substance, that the *divine originating source of all (the universe) was itself, non-matter*. This is the universally agreed conclusion of all religious persuasions, that god, the *First Cause*, is or was incorporeal spirit, or was somehow self generated from incorporeality. Some persuasions may prefer the description *incorporeal soul*, rather than incorporeal spirit; however both terms share the same basic principles of unsubstantiality, infiniteness, and timelessness. Secondly, **all religions point to this spirit god as the generator of the universe**, and many religions give detailed explanations of the exact procedures by which their gods allegedly created the universe. It amazes me how Gnostics and other religionists proclaim their religions' creationist doctrines in fantastic details, with seemingly no doubts or questions about the validity of the information or how it was obtained or witnessed. Thirdly, **all religions claim that this earthly life is not the final stage of our existence**, but rather is a stage, or phase of transit for the spirit/soul to a greater more fulfilling existence as immortal souls. All religions unanimously claim that this earthly life is an interlude. All state that our immortal souls are being either tested or punished through this temporal worldly existence, that the destiny of life is struggle - or in other words a means of purification or qualification, if not disqualification, for greater lives as spiritual beings. And fourthly, **all religions make the identical claim that salvation for our souls is reunion with god,** whether as assimilation of our individual souls into oneness with the grand *universal soul,* which is, of course god; or through special deliverance - to assembly with god in heaven/paradise in the hereafter after god's judgment and destruction of the wicked or nonbelievers. If we believe the religionists, the ultimate purpose of life is to find salvation – and what is salvation? Salvation is finding our way back to our spiritual source, god. And what will we do when we get back to god? Well, we will conquer death, and live forever. **So, it seems** that all religions are focused on giving us a means of dealing with our certain mortality by teaching that death is not real, but rather a doorway to new eternal life. There's an old saying: "everybody wants to go to heaven, but nobody wants to die"; I think that we should repeat this adage to ourselves continuously until the portent of it sinks in to our consciousness.

From the above, it is made clear – the common thread that runs through all religions is the belief that we humans are, in essence, spiritual beings; that our physical bodies are merely containers, houses, or temples in which reside our individual souls; and further that our individual souls are immortal and capable of life independent of the physical body. This belief i.e. immortality of the individual soul is the basic generally accepted assumption or presumption common to all religions of note. All religions deal with providing a route to salvation for the human soul, and all religions agree that salvation for the soul is *reunion* with the source of its generation, which is alleged to be god. The alleged cycle or *journey of the soul* then, according to Gnostic and other religious doctrines, commences as incorporeal spirit, falls or otherwise enters into matter (human bodies), where it undergoes various trials and tests pursuant to purification, reemerges from matter and circles back to the point of its origin, which is with god – and the term that describes a successful completion of this journey of the soul is called *Salvation*.

So the task that confronts us is to determine intellectually whether or not this *assumption* of the immortality of the soul, *as commonly perceived*, has factual merit. If we can successfully prove that the *cycle* of the soul, from incorporeal spirit into matter and back to spirit again, is actually a symbolism of an underlying reality, or presumed reality, we will in the same stroke invalidate this cherished false assumption – which we must do in order to lay grounds for the genuine but lost (or buried) truth of the Ancients. But if we nullify this cherished universally accepted concept of immortality - what are we left with! Our goal is to find the beacon of truth and to follow it wherever it leads us, without preference. This popular concept of immortality proposed by the Gnostics and others was not the only concept that the Ancients assiduously studied – it was the concept that won the most general acceptance, and filtered its way into the fabrics of all the worlds religious systems. The other major concept remains in the philosophical records, and may yet be observed by a few scattered groups - we shall resurrect it and discuss it in due course, within this chapter; **but our immediate task, which follows, is to unveil the underlying reality upon which the symbolism of the Journey of the Soul is patterned.**

Lifting The Gnostic Veil

I think it is clear by reason of the explanations and comparisons that I have previously noted above, that all religions base their doctrines on identical or similar unfounded and invalid assumptions. In terms of cultural influences, I am sure that most enlightened scholars would agree that this *unity of error* is traceable in part to the evolution of spirituality (animism) among the earliest primitives of yesteryear, groping in prehistorical ignorance, and bewildered by the volatile, potent, and inscrutable forces of nature. They sought to explain the generation of these forces in basic ways compatible with the dearth of their scientific understanding - they imagined that nature's forces were being manipulated by invisible beings, spirits that entered into the bodies of the winds, the seas, the stars, the trees, the plants, everything including themselves; and from these primitive animistic beginnings sprung our beliefs in invisible and fleeting spirits, fairies, phantoms, ghouls, demons, and ghosts. And when religion evolved after many millennia, the demons and spirits of our primitive beginnings became the angels, archons, immortal souls, gods, devils, good spirits and evil spirits lodged within the fabrics of our evolving religious doctrines. But we must go beyond this basic cultural explanation for an understanding of the fundamental, detailed tenets of Gnosticism, and religion in general. We must explore the physical realities or perceptions after which Gnostic doctrine is mythologically patterned, and thereby unveil the mysteries symbolized by the mythical journey of the soul, from spirit into matter and back into spirit again.

Universal Egg

Spirits based on physics is the key to unfolding great religious truths, as I have repeated so many times in my writings. As we pursue our efforts to link the symbolism of the mythological journey of the soul with the physical reality or perceived reality that it represented, we must envision the universe as the Ancients originally perceived it, before they gained, after many, many millennia, more accurate concepts of cosmic architecture. Primitive mankind thought that they were the only intelligent beings in the universe, and they thought that the world was flat – they did not understand gravity and the solar system accurately. The easiest most understandable concept of the universe that they envisioned was that the world was flat, and that all of those myriad cosmic lights that seemed to revolve around their land were indeed doing just that, revolving around their location which they believed sat at the center of the universe. They initially saw the earth as a flat plain with the sky shaped as a dome, above and below the earth, that covered and contained the earth within this egg shaped universe. They imagined that the stars, planets, and sun, revolved around their earthly plain just as the moon actually does circle our planet. We now know that the cosmos is populated by billions of planets, stars, and galaxies flying in their orbits, incalculable light years from us, and each other; but the Ancients saw all the heavenly lights as servants of man – placed in the heavens by the father god in order to light the way of man and to provide man with the means to track time. They thought the stars were linked (attached) to the orbit of the heavenly dome that they imagined enclosed the universe, that they, the stars, were at the same level with each other, and formed the boundary of the universe which separated it (the universe) from the *unknown*. They noticed the *wandering* stars and counted them, and called them planets – at the lowest level they noted the moon - than after the moon in ascending order, they counted Mercury, Venus, the Sun, Mars, Jupiter, and finally Saturn. They pictured the courses of the planets as they seemingly revolved around the earthly plain, as tracing divisions in the universe, that each planetary orbit was actually the sphere or realm or domain of that planet which it accordingly ruled and controlled. They called the planets *Powers*, and divided them into lower powers and higher powers. They taught that the sun, in the fourth position ascending from the earthly plain was the *center of the cosmic powers*, and that the planets below the sun were the *lower powers* while the planets above the sun were classified as the *higher powers*. Accordingly they also referenced these planetary divisions of the cosmos as heavens, and in total they became the seven heavens of the cosmos, and at the eighth level resided the stars, and the number nine represented infinity or the unknown. Beyond the limits of the universe, indicated by the level of the stars, they surmised that there existed a great expanse of ether or endless space, infinity, and that within that great unknown and unknowable expanse of infinity resided the creator and architect of their world.

In the above, we have given a concise explanation of how mankind saw his world thousands of years ago, while yet pagan, before the development of his more refined religious concepts. **And we contend that it was from man's *state of mind* as engendered by his perception of the universe as above depicted, and from his cultural proclivities as they pertained to the spiritual animation (animism) of natural forces, as referenced above** – it was from this basis that his religious theories were surmised and formed, thereby establishing the mythological foundation or prototype from which our modern theological precepts were subsequently developed and evolved. Our religious ideas did not spring from a vacuum, but rather our religious conceptions were engendered from the *knowledge base* and *experiences* of our progenitors – it can be no other way; unless you truly believe in godly revelations to so-called prophets, and if that be the case, we are not on the same page.

As mankind began to theorize on higher concepts of god, he used his *perceptions* of the physical universe as a reference by which to pattern his thoughts of his deity. He looked to the physical heavens, and imagined that the spiritual heavens were in parallel to that which was physical or that the physical heavens was a great expanse that separated him from the *outer limits* in which his creator resided. He pictured the aforementioned spheres of the planets, that divided the universe into sections, as cosmic stepping-stones or as an ascending stairway or heavenly ladder, which ascended into the domain of the unknown, the domain of the unknown god. He viewed the planets and the tracks of their orbits as angels or archons, or guardians that guarded the pathways or approaches to the unseen god that sat upon a throne beyond the stars. Note the following biblical passage in reference to Jacob's ladder which clearly indicates the position of god's kingdom or heaven at the outer limits of the universe that is to say above the dome of the night sky, as perceived by the Ancients: *Genesis28:10-*[10]*And Jacob went out from Beersheba, and went toward Haran. -Genesis 28:12 through Genesis28:13-*[12]*And he dreamed, and behold a ladder set up on the earth, and the top of it reached to heaven: and behold the angels of God ascending and descending on it.* [13]*And, behold, the LORD stood above it, ...*

Have no doubt about it; this flawed perception of the cosmic structure (along with inputs from primitive animism), with man in the earthly plains below, and the great expanse of the heavenly vault above, and beyond the heavenly dome shielded in perpetual obscurity the divine unknowable god, seated upon his throne as creator and ruler – this misperception of the natural order is the nexus, the foundation, the primal source of all the misconstrued theological doctrines relative to an immortal disembodied soul temporarily lodged within the bodies of man, and a spiritual god of the same non-substance, wherever found in religion or philosophy. The principle thesis of all religions, whether monotheistic or not, is #1: man has fallen or by some other means been separated from a higher (spiritual) state; #2: the goal must be to return to or attain to the higher spiritual state for his salvation; #3: religion provides a formula by which mankind can attain to the higher state; #4: failure to exercise said belief (beliefs) will result in mankind continuing in a state of disenfranchisement or further punishment for not reconciling to god by deeds and/or faith. **The aforementioned is the basis of all religions,** and all stems from the initial misconceptions of humankind's view of the structure of the universe - as a domed enclosure of seven tiers, beyond which existed an unknowable spiritual, intangible, universe of limitless spirit seen as heaven and god; but separated from man on earth by the huge *gulf* or expanse of the physical heavens. Spiritual Man, now resident in the earthly plains below, and now dressed in the grosses forms of matter (his human body) was seen as trapped, enslaved, or spiritually dead, and his salvation lay in finding a way home to his spiritual origins. The Greek tales of the perils, wars, and misfortunes of ancient Hellenians in their journeys and endless difficulties in finding their way home were symbolic of the human soul seeking to find its way home to the spiritual heaven from which it had fallen or otherwise been detached. This holds true also of the biblical enslavement of the Jews to Egypt, and some of their other struggles to find their way to the Promised Land. These myths, in great part, are symbolic of the *soul's struggles to reach home*, its promised land, its final salvation as pure spirit, released from matter – thus conquering death, death of the spirit in the grave of matter.

The premise within Gnosticism at the esoteric level is that the spirit is enslaved in matter; Israel's enslavement to Egypt was symbolic of this. Much of Bible/Quranic symbolism, and the Greek myths, and others are symbolic of the transitions of the soul from its spiritual home (outside of the universal egg) and the quest to return to that empyrean realm consistent with the trials and tribulations attendant thereto. So the concept of the enslavement of the spiritual soul to matter, to flesh is based on the fallacious premise that the universe is an enclosed egg with the earth at its center; consisting of seven divisions plus the stars as the 8th elevation, and the 9th the throne of god - above matter in the abode of the disembodied spirits. All religions function on the same basic premise, that is to say that this earthly life is not the ultimate expression of our individuality, that in some way this life is preparation for another spiritual life, or is punishment for some offense in a higher spiritual existence (hence fallen angels, original sin, etc). This mistaken spiritual conception is traceable to man's misinterpretation of the structure of cosmic nature. **If mankind had known** the true structure of the universe as we do today, he never would have imagined the *fall* from above to earth, hence this immortal soul concept was founded on error and the error was

Lifting The Gnostic Veil

compounded when transferred to mythology, and theology. **Even if we insist** on believing that this world was created and designed by an *external* god, there is no credible reason to believe that we were former residents of that alleged other world or are destined to reside there someday. Additionally there is the belief that evil and good spirits exist and are influential over the behavior of humans – modern science proves, beyond doubt, that the brain is the controller of man's actions and emotions. The concepts of spirits effecting the actions of humans traces to a time when man did not understand the biological connections to human behavior. All human actions and emotions are traceable to functions of the brain, not to embedded evil or good spirits.

Reconciliation to god is central to all forms of religion; and if I may be so redundant, the genesis of this spiritual attitude of reconciliation was based on a misconceived perception of the physical structure of the universe, whereas we here below are separated from the great father above and must somehow fly, as spirits, back to our spiritual ancestral home. Within monotheism the sequence is Punishment, Atonement, then Reconciliation. This sequence lies at the pyramidal center of all monotheistic philosophies. **First,** in the philosophical process of monotheism, there is disenfranchisement, the separation of the flock (humanity) from the shepherd (god) in heaven. This falling away usually comes in the form of banishment for pernicious misdoings or voluntary rebellion against divine authority, or separation for failure to hit the mark, which is the definition of sin. The net result of falling away from god (in heaven) is punishment. **Second:** in order to relieve the condition of punishment, we must atone for our sins. In order to atone for our sins, we must accomplish feats of expiation that prove our commitment and earnest desire to reconcile with god – this opens the door for religion in our lives, as a means of earning expiation (atonement). And **thirdly,** the monotheists impose rules, rituals, and deeds that we must follow and accomplish as a means to obtaining a hearing before god or his agents

Lifting The Gnostic Veil

pursuant to a writ of atonement; and beyond this stage we are ushered into Judgment, whereas our actions and/or faith are evaluated or judged so as to determine whether or not we are worthy for reconciliation or reunion with god. The above is central to monotheistic theology, that is to repeat – we are in a state of separation from the divine, and this state of separation is tantamount to punishment. In consequence, we must atone (by submitting to monotheistic dogma) and thereby we may earn reconciliation (reunion) with our creator god.

This is the primary focus of monotheism, and the other major religious forms, that is to say they all advocate or promise reunion or reconciliation with god as salvation. The purpose of their numerous religious rituals and codes is to facilitate the objective of reconciliation with our creator. All of the earth's major religions and mysticisms proclaim that our present lives are subordinated to higher spiritual forms or realities. They all claim that this life is some type of trial or punishment, and/or interlude, that god or salvation awaits us in another realm, and that there are various rituals, prayers, or actions that we must perform in order to qualify for passage to spiritual salvation. This stems from the universal belief in an afterlife in which our souls survive, although our bodies perish. They claim that the journey of the soul is such that this life is only a stop along the way; and if we (our souls) are to continue or return to eternal companionship with god, we must follow their various recommendations or else risk eternal damnation, or endless cycles of reincarnation into matter.

Immortality Of The Soul

There can be no doubt that the universal soul is immortal – because it *must* be immortal. If the universal soul was not immortal, all life would cease to exist. The universal soul, by whatever name we may call it, is the source of our being, the animator of our spirits. The programmed knowledge or intelligence of all things lies resident within the omnipresent, amorphous, indefinable fabric of the universal soul. And

The Meaning Of The Gnosis
31

this soul, by whatever name we may call it, be that Nature, Spirit, God, Maya, Christ, Brahman, or Life Force, or whatever is the underpinning of all that is. The soul is the source of our intelligence – all knowledge comes from the universal soul. That which we call learning is, in reality, an excavation process by which we dislodge knowledge from the universal soul secluded within our being, and bring into the awareness of our conscious soul. The universal soul is immanent within us, and within all things, biological and mineral, according to the Ancients. Nothing can *be* without the direction of the universal soul to form it and sustain it (hold it) in whatever image it projects. And all things that be (exist) were called into existence – to perform a function, a function deemed worthy or required by the immortal soul, and this includes human intelligence. All life is cause and effect.

But our concern is not only with the universal soul and its immortality – we beg to find the destiny of our own personal souls, the paths to our personal immortalities. First off, we must understand that our personal soul is our conscious mind. That which gives us awareness of our individuality is our personal soul, our temporal soul. But the conscious soul is only a part, a small fraction of what and who we really are. Our personal soul is our window to the world, our communicator, the means by which we network with each other and the environment, a tool by which we gather sustenance, and procreate, and so forth. It is the *inner soul* that drives us, and compels us in certain directions, that in some respects acts independently of the conscious soul – in fact some of the Ancients taught that we have layers of souls ingrained within our being, but I will not pursue that issue at this time. The immortal soul that is resident within us is not an independent spirit, but rather an ingrained blended part of our reality though not our consciousness. The immortal soul lives in matter, feeds on matter, and expresses itself through matter – it *needs* matter in order to perpetuate its immortality. The greatest marriage of all is the marriage between spirit and matter, that fuses them into one – on this marriage our lives depend. The second greatest marriage is the marriage between the *conscious soul* and the *universal soul* immanent within our being. This marriage, which requires great courage and desire, I am told, is consummated when the conscious soul discovers and treads the dark and hidden path that leads to *conscious spiritual awareness* and *unity* with the immortal soul resident within our being - an achievement described by some as nirvana, illumination, or enlightenment.

Spirit and matter are two parts of one whole, and although matter decays, the spirit (or immortal soul) lives on through succeeding generations of reconstituted matter. The soul is *physically* transferred from parent bodies to their offspring – philosophers call this process **Traducianism.** If we refer to the conscious mind as the conscious soul, this will help clarify our thinking in regards to the soul of man. The conscious soul rides upon the inner soul or we may say that it projects from the inner soul. It is the internal or non-conscious soul that is immortal, and the way to verify this is to contact the inner soul (hence nirvana, union) – of course most of us will never accomplish this. We contend that the only logical explanation of the existence of the soul in man is that the soul is physically *inheritable* as indicated philosophically under the banner of *Traducianism*. The concept of souls as external immortal beings temporarily housed in man is clearly flawed and without *logical or scientific* foundation. The concept is derived from man's misconception of the structure of the universe, that is the belief, that the universe was limited in size and surrounded by ether or a spiritual domain that was the original home of our souls. This is an old primitive concept born in ignorance that unfortunately has not been improved upon in thousands of years but clearly has no foundation in fact. The concept is *not* accurately reflective of physical nature, which is the paradigm that I use to define the correctness of spiritual applications.

The ancient concept of the Greeks and others was that the soul descended from heaven through seven lower plains, and as the soul fell through each level it became heavier with matter, and concurrently lost knowledge of the higher plains. They taught that the lowest plain was earth, hell, a place of trial, punishment, and purification, and that our souls are trapped in these earthly forms of matter until they qualify to re-ascend toward god. Each level of ascension of the seven spiritual plains presents its own trials that must be overcome in the journey back to our souls' heavenly home with god. This basic Gnostic concept lies at the root of all major religions, and is no more than an illusion. The concept was founded (copied) on a flawed premise of the physical structure of the universe and thereby the spiritual conclusions are likewise in error. If the ancient gnosis is to be believed, souls are constantly whizzing between heaven and earth seeking out bodies in which to implant their selves so as to endure the trials of Hades. As our physical bodies die, our souls immediately seek out new shells to house them according to the proponents of this doctrine. I suppose there is also a constant stream of new souls being exiled from heaven for their sins, and must be imprisoned in earthly matter pursuant to their redemption. Ultimately, the goal of all souls, embodied in earthly matter, is to return to heaven and the loss glory of godly companionship and immortality. This concept is actually little different from the Christian, Islamic concepts of heavenly rewards, and just as much in error. The influence of Gnosticism on monotheistic religious doctrine is potent and certain.

Dualism is a primary driving force of Gnosticism, that is the belief that there are two gods, one of good spirit and the other the creator of matter, hence matter is alleged as inherently evil. The soul is the source of animation, intelligence, and direction, so the universe *must* have a soul – period. **We propose, as was proposed by some of the Ancients, that the soul is integral to matter,** that it is carried from generation to generation, hence immortality, within the folds of matter. *If one rejects this proposal*, the only other alternative is that the soul is external to matter, and if one claims that the soul is external to matter, *one must also agree that the* *soul precedes matter,* assuming that matter must have a creator - otherwise we could claim that the material world existed *before* the spirit, its creator and source of animation, intelligence, and being – *or* that the material world is the product of *another creator (god),* hence Gnostic dualism! **And further,** if one believes that the human body is possessed of a soul that is *not* integral to matter, than one *must accept* that the soul enters and exits the body concurrent or within the cycles of conception and death of the human body. And if one believes *that,* one *must* also believe, as stated above, that souls are constantly whizzing between places unknown (as they must be generated somewhere, hence the idea of heaven above the dome of the universe) and earth making incalculable entrances into and exits out of human bodies – and to what end! And are we to believe that these externally generated whizzing souls are responsible for the characters of the humans they possess, rather than the human brain[4] as confirmed by science! And being that they (religionists) claim that the soul is judged according to the actions of the human body, since the soul is allegedly the manipulator of the human body – are we to believe that absent the whizzing souls the human body would have no decent character, hence is inherently evil, again leading to an assumption of Gnosticism! This (the idea of whizzing souls) is very illogical and bizarre, and the idea of two gods (one of matter and the other of spirit) fighting over the same prize (the human soul) doesn't smack of the astute application of resources that one would expect from supreme godly Intelligence.

Soul And Body

The spirit refers to thought, concepts of the mind, the third eye of insight, *illumination – which is the only real way to see god,* if god can be seen (comprehended), that is through the minds eye, because all that appears before the physical eyes is an illusion; that is to say an interpretation of the

---

[4] Of course our character is effected by various social factors, education, and environment.

physical senses. I repeat: that which our senses see is not the ultimate reality but rather is a sensory perception (interpretation) of reality calibrated to the tone of the organism, human or otherwise, involved. If our human sensory organs were recalibrated (adjusted to different levels of perception or intensity), then, in consequence, the world would appear different to our senses, as it does to some other animals, insects, and fishes. According to our scientists, this world is perceived (sensed) differently by various categories of life. The world that we perceive is consequential to the interactions of our physical senses with the environment, and the primary motive of nature in this regard is the transmission of data to the organism that enables its functionality within its environs; hence all organisms, including human, see (perceive) an *apparent* world, limited and imaged in accordance with the capacities of their sensory organs. Some of the Ancients called this apparent world, that we perceive as real and genuine, an illusion, a veil situated between the creator and its creation, a shield between the ultimate reality of god and us i.e. his (god's) creation. This indicates that what we view as reality is, in truth, actually an interpretation made by our sensory organs, and not the true ultimate reality. The true reality can only be seen by the third eye of enlightenment, according to some, which is our salvation – or path to salvation inside the Gnosis. **Salvation is enlightenment,** being raised to *correct* higher knowledge and awareness that overcomes the illusions of this phenomenal world. The phenomenal world is a veil that hides truth (from the profane) and protects the powers of truth (from the profane). But heaven or salvation is not, and has never truly been a destination or place of habitation for the soul or body; **heaven or salvation is an elevation of the spiritual sight** (insight) into a state of awareness and correct *rational* understanding that releases us (consciously) from fear, doubt, and confusion, according to what I have learned. Correct knowledge or rational understanding of our purpose, destiny, and relationship with the Whole is the correct path to realistic salvation, that is to say a spiritual *state of mind* that transcends our base animal instincts, and connects us sagaciously with the Gnosis thereby unveiling our fit and function, as imaginative beings, connected and integral to the universal whole. The functioning minds of our physical bodies, *in this physical life*, link the powers (soul, intelligence), resident within us, to this phenomenal world. We are hosts to the spirits that are integral to our being, and we (Matter) are likewise integral to the perpetuity of the spirit, to its (spirit's) immortality, which we (as material links, hosts or carriers of the immortal spirits) share, as it (the spirit) transits from generation to generation, piggybacking on various matter forms through eternity. The soul is resident in each of us but not as an independent spirit that is undergoing some trial or test of purification; this is the fallacious belief of those who have taken the symbolic expulsion from paradise (heaven) i.e. Original Sin as genuine symbology, which it is not. The doctrine of Original Sin and other associated doctrines are flawed; our souls have not fallen from an external world into this world of matter – **our souls are integral to matter**, part of the fabric of matter, perhaps a less dense form of matter, innate to heavier matter and interdependent with heavier or grosser matter. The soul is imbedded in matter and is inseparable, or probably not viable when separated from matter, was the conclusion of many of the Ancients who endorsed the concepts of Traducianism. In fact the soul lives immortally, by attaching itself to succeeding generations of matter. Matter decays and loses life till reformulated into revived entities. Matter, according to the laws of physics as stated by our scientists is indestructible, only transformable, so matter too is immortal in a holistic sense. The spirit is immortal so long as it has matter *on* which to feed, and *in* which to express itself. We, as humans, are the highest form of spiritual expression on this planet because we have the gift of imagination, the ability to perceive beyond the bounds of our animal instincts and sensory environment, and to imagine and question the functions of the creation and the presumed creator; and we are aware of our several mortalities as conscious individual beings.

Lifting The Gnostic Veil

The premises or theories of old that identified and explained the nature of the soul were based on false assumptions concerning the nature of the universe, its structure and expanse. The spiritual speculations derived from those mistaken notions concerning the physics of the universe are therefore in error and misleading. Plato and others of his persuasion were wise, perceptive, and very rational, but their conclusions (i.e. insights into the nature and character of god) were ascertained from flawed data concerning the physical universe, hence the results of their extensive studies were distorted. The defects of their physics model (misconceptions concerning the structure of the universe) were transmitted into their spiritual speculations. The origin of all of our religious opinions are derived from ancient mankind's interaction with nature, and his associated cultural evolution – spirits based on physics, as I have repeatedly asserted in my writings. Their spiritual assumptions (relevant to the descent of souls into matter from an external spiritual world) were perfectly logical based on the science of their times, but the science (i.e. the belief that the universe was shaped as an egg, with god's domain external to it) was skewed, and this defect in their scientific outlook caused many great men of old to err in their philosophical, religious projections, which were hypothesized in symbolic reflection (i.e. mythological tales) of their perceptions of the physical universe.

We, as humans, must recognize *our limits* in the process of attempting to correctly determine the nature of the soul and its origin. **First, we must realize that the universe is one, and all within the one (universe) is connected or inter-related**, just as the cells of our brains are related to the cells of our hearts, assigned to their various tasks but related and connected to each other because all are a part of the same *one*, and of the same substance. Our scientists tell us that the universe is one substance, that the cosmic stars and *we* are made of the same stuff - **we are one**. Our brains, the tool that we use to evaluate and decipher truth, have been engineered (by god, nature) to function within the limits imposed by the one (macrocosm) – it (the brain) will not function efficiently outside of the limits of its natural habitation, which is *this* universe. The boundaries that limit the correct functioning of our brains are the parameters of time and matter. Our brains are part of this universal machine, and they (our brains) are designed specifically for interacting and computing within the constraints of this universal order, that is to say the laws of cause and effect as determined by the innate natures of time and matter. Hence, if we presume that the eternal soul of god that animates and instructs us is native to an external world not bound by the constraints of time and matter, we in consequence, have foredoomed any efforts on the part of our brains to evaluate such a metaphysical nature that presumably precedes time and matter and is not bound by the parameters under which are brains are designed to function. In fact, that was the conclusion of the Ancients, that is that the creator god was unknowable, indiscernible, and beyond the grasps of our intellect. They asserted that god's (the creator god) name was ineffable, that means that the nature of god was deemed indefinable; they couldn't name i.e. explain the nature of timelessness, and intelligence contained in insubstantiality, which is the presumed status of the creator god – existing forever without beginning or end, and nonmaterial. This we can write or say, or imagine to a certain extent but our brains cannot logically define such status – always existing but never beginning, intelligent but formless and limitless. Such is beyond human rational understanding was their conclusion.

We, as humans, can only think *inside* the box. The box that we live in and are limited by is the box delineated by the boundaries of time and matter. Time and matter are subject to universal laws, and our brains calculate with and are governed by the same laws. Our brains were designed to function within certain natural parameters and will not function (accurately calculate) outside of those natural limits. This is not to say that our brains do not possess powers that we have yet to exploit to their full potentials; but my assertion is that all of the powers of the brain, known

Lifting The Gnostic Veil

or hidden, are governed by the same universal laws of *the one* (macrocosm) - in which we are contained.

The One, the Macrocosm is the true definition of monotheism or identity of the one god, that is to say the one and only god besides whom there is no other. The modern monotheists (Jews, Christians, and Muslims) have corrupted the true spiritual meaning of monotheism as contained in the ancient gnosis. The correct form of monotheism is monism, or pantheism, according to the gnosis. The true gnosis reveals that we all are one in god, and god is *one* (the macrocosm) – *god is all and all is god*. The whole universe is god was their conclusion, that the one soul of god permeating all creation is the life and sustenance of all creation, animate and inanimate. Hence we all are connected to the same life source and are a part of the one, the only one, the all in all – the macrocosm. Just as every individual cell of our personal body belongs to the whole body, and is an inseparable part of the whole body, in terms of viability – so likewise is our individual relationship with god; *we are individual cells in the body of god* (macrocosm). Our individual spirits are connected to the one Great Spirit, as the Native Americans use to say – we (all that exist) are expressions of the divine - in body as well as in spirit, according to the old wisdom. **Our immortality and the immortality of our souls are maintained through regeneration** – some philosophers use the term **Traducianism** to explain their concepts of the birth, rebirth or migration of our souls, which concepts are very similar to my own opinion, for what it's worth. Of course, most of us desire immortality as sensory individuals with awareness of our uniqueness as separate expressions of the divine, rather then the ultimate assimilation into the one eternal soul, which some say is the consequence of individual death.

The Symbolism Of Christ

According to the tenets of Gnosticism, as expressed through Plato's version, the universe is the emanation of the unseen and unknowable god.

The Meaning Of The Gnosis
40

Lifting The Gnostic Veil

This means that god is the father of this material universe, and further that god's soul permeates this universe, giving it life and direction. What I have just noted, as assigned to Plato is the esoteric trinity. A trinity of course is a division of three parts, and we are taught within the Christian doctrine that the godhead is divided into three parts: Father, Son, and Holy Spirit. Under the Gnosis the Father is the unknowable god, the Holy Spirit is the soul of god, and the son is the union of soul (spirit) and matter. Jesus was the Son of God under this symbolism – it was mystically expressed in the bible, after the death of Jesus on the cross - see following verses:

John 19:33 through John 19:35 - [33]*But when they came to Jesus, and saw that he was dead already, they brake not his legs:* [34]*But one of the soldiers with a spear pierced his side, and forthwith came there out blood and water.* [35]*And he that saw it bare record, and his record is true: and he knoweth that he saith true, that ye might believe.*

The blood and water that came out of the body of Jesus symbolized matter and spirit, as esoterically *red* blood is the symbol of matter and *white* (clear) water is the symbol of spirit. This is universally expressed as the red devil, as Adam being made of red mud, as with baptism in the spirit being associated with *holy* water, and so forth.

Actually there are two tracks that can be taken with *this* symbolism of the trinity - that which I have already indicated, in the form of Emanationism whereas the Father (god) brings forth his son directly, out of his own spiritual substance, so that the son is identical to the Father but made visible, whereas the Father remains invisible (pure spirit) and unreachable. The other track of the symbolism shows the Father impregnating the mother (matter) of his son so that the son is born possessing the spiritual attributes of the Father though made of the substance of his earthly mother (matter). Both symbolisms refer to the union of spirit and matter, which is the composition of our universe, the macrocosm - but in the former the son is the direct image of god, while in the latter the son is

The Meaning Of The Gnosis
41

imbued with the spirit of god but not the *quality* of god. Of course this issue was hotly debated among the early Christians under the Arius controversy concerning the nature of Christ, whether he was man or god. The debate was undertaken at the exoteric level, but was underpinned, in the minds of the enlightened by the need to maintain allegorical accuracy, as they saw it. The winners of the debate, as history shows, were those whose philosophy was in accord with Plato's concept of Emanationism, as expressed in John chapter one. The Emanationist aspect is expressed in John of the bible, whereas the word (emanating spirit) is made flesh (matter):

John 1:1
[1]In the beginning was the Word, and the Word was with God, and the Word was God. **John 1:2**
[2]The same was in the beginning with God. **John 1:14-**[14]*And the Word was made flesh, and dwelt among us, (and we beheld his glory, the glory as of the only begotten of the Father,) full of grace and truth.* **John 1:18-**[18]*No man hath seen God at any time; the only begotten Son, which is in the bosom of the Father, he hath declared him.*

The above clearly refers to Jesus (The Word) as being directly emanated by the Father (unknowable god), that the spirit from within the Father was emanated out and became flesh (matter). Of course in other portions of the bible, the Father is described as placing his spirit inside matter (impregnating matter (the mother)) so that matter (the mother) brings forth a son (*her* son, anointed with the spirit of the unseen god). Of course this never happened with real people – Jesus Christ was, in truth, a symbol of the macrocosm. It is interesting – if you trace the root of the word *matter,* you find that words such as maternity, matron, matrimony, maternal, matrix, and *mother* are derived from the term *matter.* So spirit married to matter produces offspring that is the combination of both, and this is the *eternal* trinity – the merging of spirit and matter, which produces a third, which is heir and a union of both substances (parents).

The unknown god the Father is unreachable, and we must go through the son so as to reach the Father. This is basic Christian theology and is 100 % in accord with Gnostic doctrine. As I have already indicated, the son refers to the macrocosm, the universe itself - the begotten (emanated image) son of the unknowable god. Christians for the most part don't worship god, they worship Jesus, as an intermediary, and this is in accord with the symbolism. The universe itself is our witness to the glory and power of the unseen god, and stands between us, and the Creator. What we are being told under this symbolism is that the universe itself, the macrocosm is *our* god, and the force (god the father) that created or emanated his son (macrocosm, universe) is beyond our conception. Actually the correct description of Jesus is *lord*, not god. Lord means master, and that's exactly what Jesus (the macrocosm) is – he/it is our master, our governor, our ruler, the mediator that lies between us and the unknowable first cause of all things. This is the esoteric wisdom of the Ancients. Note the following biblical passages:

1-Corinthians-8:6 -[6]But to us there is but <u>one God, the Father</u>, of whom are all things, and we in him; and <u>one Lord Jesus Christ</u>, by whom are all things, and we by him.

In the above of 1st Corinthians, it is clearly conveyed that Jesus is lord, not god. Jesus, the macrocosm, is like our overlord, our ruler, the administrator for god that we must serve and obey. As we know, Jesus never lived as a human being – the biblical story is completely symbolic at several levels, astronomically, agriculturally, and culturally, as I have explained in my other writings. You will discover, I believe, that the more you study Christianity that it is a very, very old belief system that has been so grossly distorted at the exoteric level that its similarities to ancient doctrines are hardly recognizable, until discerned at the esoteric level. The esoteric explanations of Christian doctrine that we have provided prove this to be true.

Take note of the following biblical passages concerning spirit and matter, and the duality inherent within Christian theology, which are clearly Gnostic in their import:

Romans 7:22 through Romans 7:25
[22] For I delight in the law of God after the inward man: [23] But I see another law in my members, warring against the law of my mind, and bringing me into captivity to the law of sin which is in my members. [24] O wretched man that I am! who shall deliver me from the body of this death? [25] I thank God through Jesus Christ our Lord. So then with the mind I myself serve the law of God; but with the flesh the law of sin.

The verses above clearly indicate the Gnostic belief that the soul is *captive* in the body, that is to say in matter, which is pure Gnosticism, or without doubt derived from Gnosticism. Note also in the above the definition of death, that *death is the captivity of the soul* in matter. This is considered the death sentence that was assigned to the spiritual Adam per the Garden of Eden myth, and hence all human souls are under the death sentence that they inherited from the spiritual Adam - but lo, god sent Jesus to die for our sins, that is the original sin of Adam in the Garden. So if we believe in Christ, we are released from the death sentence, which as previously noted above, is captivity of the soul. That means, when this physical body of ours expires, our souls will return to heaven as redeemed by Christ. This dogma of atonement, by the death of Christ, lies at the core of Christian theology, and it is the weakest, most nonsensical aspect of the doctrine, in terms of rationality. See the following biblical quote: *1-Corinthians-15:21,through-1Corinthians-15:22-For since by man came death, by man came also the resurrection of the dead. 22For as in Adam all die, even so in Christ shall all be made alive.*

These verses from 1st Corinthians of the bible confirm that biblically, Adam is responsible for the death of our souls, and that Christ is our redeemer. I point this out for one good reason – and that is, you cannot believe literally in Christ without also believing literally in Adam and the whole fantastic tale of the Garden of Eden myth. In other words, if the Garden of Eden tale was not literally true, then the coming of Christ cannot be literally true – **because Christ's coming is predicated on the authenticity of the Garden of Eden saga.** If god did not condemn all of our souls to death because of the sins of Adam, then the foundation for the coming of Christ to redeem our souls is totally demolished. In order for the Christ myth to be authentic, the Garden of Eden tale must also be genuine, and I think that is too much for most rationally minded people to accept - as you may recall, Adam ate an apple or some fruit from the forbidden tree, after being persuaded to do so by a reptile, found out that he and his wife were naked, and so on and so on.

Within this chapter we have attempted to explain the origin and meaning of Gnostic belief systems, and their unpublished influence on all of the world's religions. We have tried to explain how and from what sources our religious notions are derived. We have introduced the term Paleo-Gnosticism, and have described it as a methodology by which mythological and religious symbolism can be *correctly* interpreted. In the next chapter, we shall give examples of this Paleo-Gnostic methodology

Chapter 2

Paleo-Gnostic Methodology Exemplified

Exploration of the cultural roots of religious symbolism, with interpretations and explanations that link the symbols with the underlying realities

Paleo-Gnostic Systems Defined

We have explained previously that Paleo-Gnosticism is the system by which religious mythology is linked with its esoteric or underlying meanings. We have asserted that mythology, the mother of religion, was the method by which the Ancients recorded and preserved their cultural, historical, astronomical, agricultural, and other vital data in encrypted language; and we have proclaimed further that Paleo-Gnosticism is the science by which this encrypted language is deciphered. The Ancients determined that allegorical tales and poems were the most efficient, secure, and reliable method by which to convey societal information from generation to generation over vast periods of history; first orally, through oral renditions, and later in written, pictorial, and other art and associated forms, including architecture, as their societies evolved and developed these various skills and techniques over the centuries. The Torah, Bible, and Quran are not true repositories of valid historical events, but rather these books are collections of various tales and myths derived from more ancient mythological documents or oral traditions. These allegorical tales carry potent cultural and scientific messages veiled in the encrypted languages of mythology. The underlying messages are primarily cultural, astronomical, and agricultural, and almost always deal with the 'correct tracking of time, so that mankind could properly and successfully navigate through the seasonal changes and various other ominous cycles that effect our planet at regular intervals. Within this chapter we shall exemplify this system of discernment i.e. Paleo-Gnosticism so as to validate, and prove our assertions, beyond reasonable or rational doubts. Of course, the reader should also reference my other writings wherein I have exemplified this system, namely the series of books titled "The Astrological Foundation of the Christ Myth" and "The Biggest Lie Ever Told, 4th Edition".

Four Horsemen Of The Apocalypse Defined

Revelation 6:1 through Revelation 6:8[1]And I saw when the Lamb opened one of the seals, and I heard, as it were the noise of thunder, one of the four beasts saying, Come and see. [2]And I saw, and behold a white horse: and he that sat on him had a bow; and a crown was given unto him: and he went forth conquering, and to conquer. [3]And when he had opened the second seal, I heard the second beast say, Come and see. [4]And there went out another horse that was red: and power was given to him that sat thereon to take peace from the earth, and that they should kill one another: and there was given unto him a great sword. [5]And when he had opened the third seal, I heard the third beast say, Come and see. And I beheld, and lo a black horse; and he that sat on him had a pair of balances in his hand. [6]And I heard a voice in the midst of the four beasts say, A measure of wheat for a penny, and three measures of barley for a penny; and see thou hurt not the oil and the wine. [7]And when he had opened the fourth seal, I heard the voice of the fourth beast say, Come and see. [8]And I looked, and behold a pale horse: and his name that sat on him was Death, and Hell followed with him. And power was given unto them over the fourth part of the earth, to kill with sword, and with hunger, and with death, and with the beasts of the earth.

The four horses represent the cardinal points of the zodiac:

The Four Horses Of the Apocalypse are identical to the four horses of ancient Greek mythology that pulled the chariot of the mythical Greek

Paleo-Gnostic Methodology Exemplified

Lifting The Gnostic Veil

god Helios. The Greek god Helios symbolized the sun, and according to Greek lore, Helios traversed the heavens daily in his chariot, pulled by four great stallions. These four horses of the Greek and other mythologies that were described as transporting the sun (typed as various symbolical personages) were designates of the four cardinal points i.e. the Vernal Equinox, the Autumnal Equinox, the Winter Solstice, and the Summer Solstice. The cardinal points were stations by which the Ancients tracked the movement of the sun; hence they sometimes symbolized those stations (cardinal points) as horses that figuratively pulled the sun across the sky from station to station. The white horse symbolizes the Vernal Equinox, the red horse symbolizes the Autumnal Equinox, the black horse symbolizes the Winter Solstice, and the pale (green) horse symbolizes the Summer Solstice. White is the color of the good spirit, and in its mythical aspects correlates astronomically to the Vernal Equinox. Red is the opposite or opponent (counterpart) of white in much of the symbolism, and represents the Autumnal Equinox. Matter is counterbalanced by spirit just as the Autumnal Equinox is counterbalanced by the Vernal Equinox, so the red horse is the Autumnal Equinox, the controller of the entrance into the infernal regions of the lower hemisphere. Black signifies the darkness of the pit of the lower world where the sun is shrouded in blackness. Green represents the verdant quality of the summer season brought in by the Summer Solstice; the bible uses the term pale horse, but all of the biblical dictionaries define the term pale as synonymous to the color green. I suspect that the editors of the bible wanted to add additional obscurity to the true import of the green horse as well as add a more sinister bent to the description, so they used the synonym "pale" instead of green to describe the horse that represents the Summer Solstice, but you need only check any reputable biblical dictionary, and my definition of *green* for the pale horse will be verified.

Lifting The Gnostic Veil

The Riders of the Four Horses of the Apocalypse

The *Riders* of the horses are distinct and separate from the horses in terms of their identity; one reason that other scholars, over the years and centuries, have failed to interpret this symbolism correctly is that they have blended the individual riders and their assigned horses into single entities, which is in error. The "Riders" of the four horses are the zodiac signs that pass (ride) over the stations of the horses (cardinal points) during the day, year, or astrological era that may be targeted by the symbolism. The descriptions of the riders give us sufficient information for their identifications: he that sat on the white horse had a bow and a crown, which indicates the sector of Sagittarius, with the bow (Kaus Australis) and the crown (Corona Australis) of that sector; he that sat on the red horse is described as a killer and a disrupter of the peace, which indicates the killer scorpion that carries the sting of death, whose venom ushers in the sorrow and misery of the winter season as the sun dips below the equinoxes into the sector of Scorpio; he that sat on the black horse carried balances in his hand, which, of course, is the scale of Libra; he that sat on the pale (green) horse was called "Death" and the governor of hell, which, of course is Satan i.e. Capricorn, the well-known goat devil of the zodiac.

The revisions (editing) of these biblical passages were done during times, circa 2,000 years ago, when the official cardinal points of that era were represented by Aries, Cancer, Libra, and Capricorn. The Vernal Equinox is the prime indicator of any given astrological era, and the other cardinal points are identified in turn by the 4th, 7th, and 10th stations, counting eastward from the sign that occupies the Vernal Equinox. The (biblical) edits were done during the years when the Vernal Equinox was situated at the cusp of Pisces and Aries, that is to say at about the 1st degree of Aries and the 30th degree of Pisces - so the designation for the era of the symbolism can be applied to Aries, even though, precessionally, we were moving into the era of Pisces.

Paleo-Gnostic Methodology Exemplified

Lifting The Gnostic Veil

Since the earth rotates on its axis daily, we pass under all twelve of the zodiac signs within twenty-four hours of time; also since the earth revolves completely around the sun in one year, the sun appears to pass through all of the zodiac signs, from Aries to Pisces, annually; also, by reason of the precession of the equinoxes, the sun passes through all twelve of the zodiac signs over a period of 25,920 years. The Ancients wrote symbolisms pertaining to all three of the aforementioned cycles i.e. the Daily Cycle of 24 hours, the Annual Cycle of 360 plus days, and the Precessional Cycle of 25,920 years. I have uncovered interpretations of the Apocalyptic Four Horsemen applicable to all of the cycles just noted; but I shall focus, at this time, on interpretations relevant to the annual cycle - interpretations, which are very intriguing and expansive.

The Book Of Revelation is focused on the Last Days, also called the Judgment Days; therefore, in consequence of this focus on perdition, they (the editors) have directed our attention to those *signs in the heavens* (zodiac signs) that signal, most significantly, the End Times (Judgment Days). The Four Horsemen Of The Apocalypse usher in the Last Days, according to the biblical accounts; they are the harbingers of Judgment Day. It is important and significant that we note that the horses (cardinal points) upon which the horsemen ride should not be viewed with dread, but rather the horsemen (constellations) themselves should be viewed as portentous. The zodiacal signs that they (four horsemen) represent, are the true indicators of the terrors of the Last Days, *not* the four horses (cardinal points). Chapter six of Revelation makes it abundantly clear that the "Riders" (zodiac signs) that sat upon the horses are indicators of the terrible horrors and afflictions associated with the final Judgment, but the horses (cardinal points) are merely points of reference by which the constellations are transiently associated; actually all twelve of the zodiac signs ride (pass over) the cardinal points, in turn, during the course of the year. The primary esoteric objective of the editors of the bible, in their promotion of the tale of the Apocalyptic Four Horsemen, was to acquaint us and remind us (the enlightened) of those zodiacal constellations that signal The Last Days; and what are the Last Days! The Last Days of the annual cycle is the period of the year that governs the transition from the summer season of growth and plenty to the winter season of dearth and need. Again, the Ancients symbolically identified the ominous and foreboding constellations of the Apocalypse as Sagittarius, Scorpio, Libra, and Capricorn; Sagittarius rode upon the white horse, which signified the Vernal Equinox; Scorpio rode upon the red horse, which signified the Autumnal Equinox; Libra rode upon the black horse, which signified the Winter Solstice; and Capricorn rode upon the pale (green) horse, which signified the Summer Solstice.

The forenamed constellations are actually the 7th through the 10th signs of the zodiac, and this fact is key; their proper sequence is Libra, Scorpio, Sagittarius, and Capricorn. Libra, as the 7th zodiacal constellation, is the sign that heralds the fall of the sun beneath the equinoxes; this sign indicates the beginning of the End, the Last Days. As we learned earlier, the mythological *judgments* take place at the equinoxes, either the vernal or the autumnal, depending on the focus of the symbolism. In the mythology, the lower hemisphere, charted by the zodiacal constellations Libra, Scorpio, Sagittarius, Capricorn, Aquarius, and Pisces signal perdition while the upper portion of the zodiac, the Northern Hemisphere, charted by Aries, Taurus, Gemini, Cancer, Leo, and Virgo signal salvation. The lower constellations are usually symbolized as the Sea or the Wilderness, and the upper constellations are usually symbolized as the Land or the Earth in many cases. When the sun or any star or asterism hovers either equinox, it is positioned mythologically upon the Sea and the Earth: note Revelation, Chapter 10 *"[5]And the angel which I saw **stand upon the sea and upon the earth** lifted up his hand to heaven";* this is, of

---

[5] According to the biblical dictionaries, the word angel means messenger; under mythical symbolism, an angel could be any celestial entity, a planet, asterism, star, etc.

course, figurative language, and we should not strain our brains, trying to visualize such events literally, but rather seek the truth by attempting to accurately interpret the symbolism. The equinoxes are transition points between the upper and lower hemispheres, hence all celestial entities that cross those points (equinoxes) are, at the times of their crossings, situated (straddling or standing) upon the Sea and the Earth. These four constellations (Libra, Scorpio, Sagittarius, and Capricorn) constitute *one-third* of the signs of the zodiac, which is very significant within biblical allegory, and these four signs are the true harbingers of Judgment signified within biblical mythology. Please note this quote from *The Astrological Foundation Of The Christ Myth Book Four*, concerning the Apocalypse or Final Judgment: "*Let us review another correlation that encompasses the Feasts of the Fall season or the autumnal equinox. The book of Revelations is full of ominous portent. Revelations is an apocalyptic rendition of the symbolism – one reason for this is that much of Revelations pertains to the symbolism of the autumnal equinox. The Fall festivals are the feasts of Judgment within the Jewish culture. The first feast of the Fall season (the 5ᵗʰ of the 7 yearly Feasts), Rosh Hashanah i.e. New Years is called Judgment Day by the Jews. The astrological sign of Libra (the 7ᵗʰ zodiacal sign) is the zodiacal symbol of justice – the scales represent the weighing of deeds and actions and the determination of justice as a result*". Judgment begins at the Autumnal Equinox and it ends at the Vernal Equinox in the phase of the symbolism we are reviewing. Judgment Day is not actually a day, but rather a number of days; it is a period of natural transition, from the agreeable weather of summer (experienced while the sun is above the equinoxes) to the inclement weather of winter (while the sun is below the equinoxes); the end of Judgment results in Deliverance, which is when the sun completes its trek through the Valley Of Death i.e. the Underworld, and returns to the Northern Hemisphere in Spring, proximate to the Passover Feast. Of course, when the sun rises through the gate of the Vernal Equinox, and enters the Northern Hemisphere, it brings the salvation of a warm and productive climate to the inhabitants of earth. The biblical tales regarding

Judgment Day are actually symbolical renditions of seasonal transitions, from summer to winter and back to summer again, in many cases

Draconis, the Great Dragon

Libra, Scorpio, Sagittarius, and Capricorn are the Four Horsemen of the Apocalypse, without doubt, and the Judgment Day(s) that is ushered in by their coming is the judgment accompanying the sun's fall below the equinoxes into the hells of the astronomical underworld. This is further evidenced by other portions of the Bible; note these passages from Chapter 12 of Revelation: *"³And there appeared another wonder in heaven; and behold a great red dragon, having seven heads and ten horns, and seven crowns upon his heads. ⁴And **his tail drew the third part of the stars of heaven,**"* We are told by these verses of the Bible that the Dragon's tail drew a *third part* of the stars of heaven. This symbolism points directly to the zodiacal signs Libra, Scorpio, Sagittarius, and Capricorn, which are situated right in the fold of the Dragon's tail. I have explained, conclusively, in Book Four[6] that the Dragon of the apocalyptic heavens of the Bible symbolizes the constellation Draconis, within the stellar symbolism. The tail of the biblical Dragon of the Heavens in the Bible is synonymous to the tail of the cosmic Dragon, which is, in fact, the constellation Draconis. The constellation of Draconis stretches over nearly half of the skies Celestial Longitude, and at the time of the biblical editing, the tail of Draconis traversed the span of the zodiac stretching from the autumnal equinox through the winter solstice - a span of four zodiac constellations thus denoting the fall of the sun into the lower regions of the cosmos, as demarcated by the celestial equator. **The sectors of Libra, Scorpio, Sagittarius, and Capricorn governed, or perhaps I should say marked, the entrance of the sun into the underworld, the region of judgment**. Two thousand years ago, when the Bible was edited, the sign

---

[6] That is *The Astrological Foundation of the Christ Myth Book Four*

of **Libra** was positioned in the 12th to the 14th hour of Right Ascension, **Scorpio** was positioned in the 14th to the 16th hour of Right Ascension, **Sagittarius** was positioned in the 16th to the 18th hour of Right Ascension, and **Capricorn** was positioned in the 18th to the 20th hour of Right Ascension. The 12th hour of Right Ascension, where the celestial equator and ecliptic intersect, marks the position of the Autumnal Equinox, and we know that this position signals the fall of the sun into the regions of the cosmic hell, defined astronomically as the southern hemisphere – also, allegorically, the sinking of the sun below the equinoxes signifies Judgment Day in the phase of the mythology that we are presently reviewing. **From the 12th to the 20th hour translates into 120 degrees of Right Ascension**, one Hour-Circle spans fifteen degrees; 120 degrees is 1/3 the total circumference of the heavens, which totals 360 degrees. **The four sectors** of Libra, Scorpio, Sagittarius, and Capricorn equate therefore to 1/3 i.e. *the third part* of the stars of heaven, described, with apocalyptic flavor, in Chapter 12 of Revelation. Take note of the graphic on the next picture page, which provides a Mercator Projection of the sectors under review, that depicts the heavens of the Draconis region, as it appeared, at the commencement of the Pisces era. The graphic clearly shows that the tail of the cosmic Draconis runs lateral to the four horsemen (constellations) of the biblical Apocalypse, and that those four constellations (Libra, Scorpio, Sagittarius, and Capricorn) were situated, successively, below the celestial equator 2000 years ago when the mythology of the Bible was last updated (edited). **The 12th hour of the zodiac, which is the point of intersection between the celestial equator and the ecliptic of the sun,** is the point where the sun descends into the regions of hell, and this transition symbolizes Judgment Day within the mythology. These four sectors comprise one-third of the cosmos, thus the Ancients described the sectors as containing one-third of the stars of heaven; they were referring to the actual astronomical heavens and not to an unseen spiritual heaven populated with unseen angels and demons. This is vivid!

Lifting The Gnostic Veil

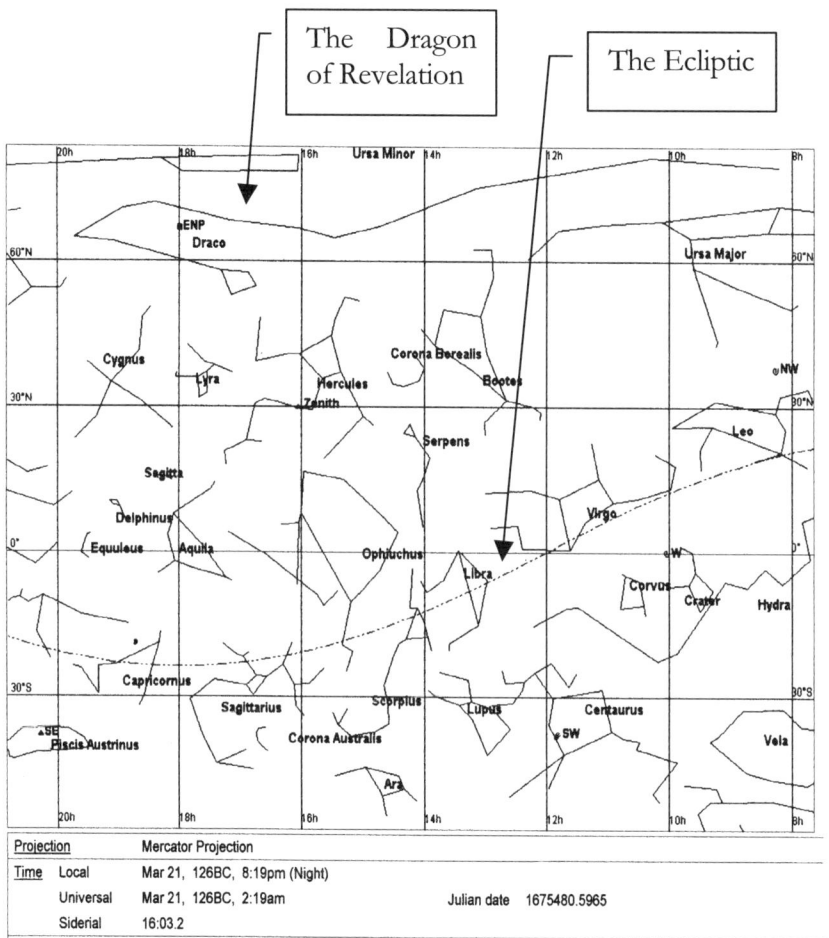

Figure 1: Note the Dragon (Draco) near top of graphic, spanning almost 6 sectors, note curved line about 2/3 down is ecliptic i.e. path of the sun, note positions of Libra, Scorpius, Sagittarius, and Capricorn, spanning from 12th to 20th hours; these 4 sectors include 1/3 of the stars of heaven (cosmic heaven), and run lateral to the tail of Draco (the Dragon of Revelation)

Paleo-Gnostic Methodology Exemplified

Lifting The Gnostic Veil

So we have clearly explained in the above that the Four "Horsemen" Of the Apocalypse actually refer to the four zodiacal constellations that mark the transitions from the pleasant and amenable summer season into the oppressive climate of winter. The Ancients symbolized this period of seasonal change, the harbinger of environmental dread and suffering, as a form of judgment. This allegory of the Four Horsemen is very strong symbolism. As I indicated above, I have successfully interpreted this symbolism at three levels of the gnosis, which includes a period of adversity cycled within the span of the Great Year of precession, 25,920 years – but we will not focus on that advanced interpretation at this time. The Bible, Quran, and other writings of the Ancients contain much parallel symbolism, symbolism applicable to multiple cycles, such as lunar, solar, stellar, seasonal, agricultural, diurnal, annual, and various multiyear cycles spanning ultimately into millions of years - as well as much cultural symbolism. **Our main focus, at this time is the annual cycle**, but in due course we shall also explore the cycle of the *Great Year at 25,920* years and also the cycle which I describe as the *Great Cycle of Axis Rotation* which spans 2,160,000 years. I shall explain and prove the Great Cycle of Axis Rotation within this book.

Noah's Ark And The Deluge Defined

Genesis 7:1 And the LORD said unto Noah, Come thou and all thy house into the ark; for thee have I seen righteous before me in this generation.

Genesis 7:4 For yet seven days, and I will cause it to rain upon the earth forty days and forty nights; and every living substance that I have made will I destroy from off the face of the earth.

Genesis 7:6 And Noah was six hundred years old when the flood of waters was upon the earth.

Genesis 7:10 through Genesis 7:11 And it came to pass after seven days, that the waters of the flood were upon the earth.

Paleo-Gnostic Methodology Exemplified

[11]*In the six hundredth year of Noah's life, in the second month, the seventeenth day of the month, the same day were all the fountains of the great deep broken up, and the windows of heaven were opened.*

Genesis7:17[7]*And the flood was forty days upon the earth; and the waters increased, and bare up the ark, and it was lift up above the earth.*

Genesis7:24[24]*And the waters prevailed upon the earth an hundred and fifty days.*
Genesis8:3throughGenesis8:5[3]*And the waters returned from off the earth continually: and after the end of the hundred and fifty days the waters were abated.*

[4]*And the ark rested in the seventh month, on the seventeenth day of the month, upon the mountains of Ararat.* [5]*And the waters decreased continually until the tenth month: in the tenth month, on the first day of the month, were the tops of the mountains seen.*

Genesis8:6throughGenesis8:13[6]*And it came to pass at the end of forty days, that Noah opened the window of the ark which he had made:* [7]*And he sent forth a raven, which went forth to and fro, until the waters were dried up from off the earth.* [8]*Also he sent forth a dove from him, to see if the waters were abated from off the face of the ground;* [9]*But the dove found no rest for the sole of her foot, and she returned unto him into the ark, for the waters were on the face of the whole earth: then he put forth his hand, and took her, and pulled her in unto him into the ark.* [10]*And he stayed yet other seven days; and again he sent forth the dove out of the ark;* [11]*And the dove came in to him in the evening; and, lo, in her mouth was an olive leaf plucked off: so Noah knew that the waters were abated from off the earth.* [12]*And he stayed yet other seven days; and sent forth the dove; which returned not again unto him any more.*

[13]*And it came to pass in the six hundredth and first year, in the first month, the first day of the month, the waters were dried up from off the earth: and Noah removed the covering of the ark, and looked, and, behold, the face of the ground was dry.*

Lifting The Gnostic Veil

Noah was a calendar, not a person

The biblical passages listed above, from Genesis of the Bible, relate the well-known Noah myth. **The story of Noah is pure mythology**; it has no basis in actual history whatsoever; it is not, as some think, an inflated legendary account of an actual historical or pre-historical event. **Noah never lived** and the biblical flood never occurred literally, i.e. not as depicted in the Bible, and not in any way similar to the narrative of the Bible. The Noachian saga is astronomical mythology, and the term Noah actually refers to a chronological system, a method of measuring the annual cycle of the sun. The primary astronomical coordinates and cosmic cycles used as references by the Noah adherents were the equinoxes, solstices, and cycles of the moon. Some think that because of the plethora of flood legends that crosses many ancient cultures, that validity is therefore accrued to the Noah myth as an actual historical event, muddled by time - but this assumption is in error. This is not to say that various cultures of the distant and pre-historic past have not experienced devastating floods that decimated their societies; the point that I must stress, and will shortly prove, is that the Noachian saga, itself, is not related to any actual earthly flood, at all.

Our interpretation of the Noah myth will prove the assertion we have made above, beyond all reasonable doubt. **First**, We shall offer an overview of Noachian saga along with insights as to its true meaning, **and secondly** we shall provide detailed, mathematical, and astronomical proofs of our contentions. According to the Noah tale, God became angry with humanity because of corruption, and therefore decided to kill every living soul on the planet, save Noah and his family: ***Genesis6:11 through Genesis6:13*** *[11]The earth also was corrupt before God, and the earth was filled with violence. [12]And God looked upon the earth, and, behold, it was corrupt; for all flesh had corrupted his way upon the earth. [13]And God said unto Noah, The end of all flesh is come before me; for the earth is filled with violence through them; and, behold, I will destroy them with the earth.* As the story goes, God told Noah to build a

Paleo-Gnostic Methodology Exemplified

boat and load it with two or seven of every type land animal and creeping thing that inhabited the planet; please note: the total area of the earth, land and water, is approximately 200,000,000 square miles, the water area is approximately 140,000,000 square miles, and the land is approximately 60,000,000 square miles; so if we accept the Bible as literally true, we must accept, as fact, that Noah scoured every island, mountain, desert, continent, cave, valley, the Artic regions, all the swamps, and forests, and whatever and wherever; and subsequently loaded into his boat an assortment of creatures from every region of our planet. How any rational mind accept this as fact is beyond my comprehension! The Bible states categorically, in Genesis 7:21-24, that every land creature on the planet was killed by the flood, except for those that were lodged with Noah; this tale is obviously mythological, and unfounded in fact. I also find it very interesting that, according to the Bible, this destruction was wrought by God against human kinds because of their corruption; however, the corruption practiced by humanity before the Flood, and after the Flood, on up to this very day, is comparable – so where lies the logic, and god's omnipotent foresight!

The keys to the proper and correct interpretation of the Noachian saga lay in the numbers; the saga begins on Noah's 600th birthday. **The first phase** of time indicated by the Bible was seven days, followed by forty days of rain, which takes us to the second month and the 17th day of the month, which concurrently is the second month and seventeenth day of the 600th year of Noah's life: ***Genesis 7:11 through Genesis 7:12*** [11]*In the six hundredth year of Noah's life, in the second month, the seventeenth day of the month, the same day were all the fountains of the great deep broken up, and the windows of heaven were opened.* [12]*And the rain was upon the earth forty days and forty nights.* I must repeat: Noah was not a person, but rather a calendar. **The next phase** spans 150 days (***Genesis 7:24*** [24]*And the waters prevailed upon the earth an hundred and fifty days)*; one hundred and fifty days is equivalent to five months at thirty days per month; this takes us to the seventh month and the seventeenth day of the month. The 17th day of the 7th month is the 1st full moon following the Vernal Equinox, according to the Jewish calendar; this is key to unraveling the mystery of the Noah calendar. **The next phase** spans 73 days and takes us to the tenth month and the first day of the month i.e. the New Moon of the 10th month; this is proximate to the Summer Solstice: ***Genesis 8:4 through Genesis 8:5*** *[4] And the ark rested in the seventh month, on the seventeenth day of the month, upon the mountains of Ararat. [5] And the waters decreased continually until the tenth month: in the tenth month, on the first day of the month, were the tops of the mountains seen.* I derived the period of 73 days by subtracting the span of *7 months plus 17 days* from the *10th month and 1st day*, mentioned in the preceding biblical verses. We know that the 10th month marks the Summer Solstice by using simple arithmetic, that is by adding 7 + 40 + 150 + 73 = 270 days. The symbolic year[7] of the Hebrews, under Noachian chronology began at the Autumnal Equinox, and includes 360 days (degrees) for the year, divided into four equal sectors of 90 days (degrees) each, so the Summer Solstice fell about 270 days into the calendar in-keeping with the annual cycle.

Noachian calendar preceded the Mosaic calendar

The Noachian calendar was the calendar used by the Hebrews *before* they adopted their modern calendar, that is to say, the Mosaic calendar. The Moses calendar evolved from or was spawned by the myth relating to the Hebrew slavery and liberation from Egypt. The Moses calendar is a lunar calendar that incorporates the Metonic System so as to correlate lunar time with solar time, and also includes several festival dates as reminders of agricultural activities. All of the agricultural festivals were *not* included in the Noah calendar. The Noachian calendar predated the Mosaic

---

[7] The Symbolic Year is a year of 360 days. In some of their solar and stellar symbolisms, the Ancients referenced the year as 360 days in order to facilitate computations, and to correlate the days of the years to the degrees of a circle (cycle). Nevertheless they also, by various methods, kept track of the actual tropical year of 365 – 366 days.

calendar, and therefore the Mosaic calendar (a more developed calendar) contains more festival dates and other information than the earlier Noachian calendar, especially as related to agriculture. The calendar fashioned under the name of the mythological Moses was more focused on lunar timekeeping than the earlier, antediluvian calendar that prevailed under the mythical Noah. The Noah calendar was a hybrid type, balanced somewhere in between the lunar and solar cycles – it copied the Egyptian calendar. Over time the Noah calendar gave way to the calendar that was later developed from the Mosaic mythology, and evidently the earlier Noah calendar was not as accurate, or user-friendly, as the Moses Calendar. The Moses calendar incorporates the Metonic system; the Metonic cycle correlates lunar time to solar time at intervals of nineteen years. The Hebrew year commences in the fall proximate to the Autumnal Equinox; this is their Rosh Hashanah (New Years, Tishri 1). The Hebrew year contains twelve months: Tishri, Heshvan, Kislev, Tevet, Shevat, Adar, Nisan, Iyar, Sivan, Tammuz, Av, and Elul. **It is important** to note that under the Noachian calendar, their months did not alternate between 29 and 30 days, as with the current Jewish calendar, but were all months of 30 days each – this is key (the lost key, overlooked by so many before now) to the unfolding of the Noachian calendar symbolism. Under the Noachian calendar, the Hebrews counted their years as solar years of 360 days plus five uncounted days, and *not* as lunar years of approximately 354 lunar days, as they now do under the Mosaic calendar (current Jewish calendar that incorporates the Metonic system).

So far, the Bible has supplied us with three cardinal points and three lunar dates with which those solar/stellar coordinates were associated: the Autumnal Equinox, that is proximate to the 1st day of the month and year of the Noah calendar; the Vernal Equinox, that is proximate to the 17th day and 7th month of the Noah calendar; the Summer Solstice, that is proximate to the 1st day and 10th month of the Noah calendar. The Bible also notes the 2nd month and the 17th day of the month, which is about

Lifting The Gnostic Veil

40-47 days past the Autumnal Equinox, or, more accurately, about 40 days past the New Moon that marked the first day of the first month of the Hebrew year, which was the New Moon most proximate to the Autumnal Equinox. This biblical date (17th day of the 2nd month) is proximate to our present day Halloween and some other European festivals that mark the completion of the span of seasonal transition. The forty days rain that precipitated the *cosmic* Noah Flood referred to the transitional period of forty days, as the sun sank progressively lower into the southern hemisphere. We know that seasonal changes are not instant, but rather seasons tend to merge from one season into the other; this transitional period takes forty days to finalize itself. The Ancients observed that the sun's impact upon the earthly environment was not immediate as it transited the cardinal points in turn, but rather transitional, for a period covering 40 days, before the next season was firmly seated. From Noah's birthday to the 10th month i.e. 1st day of the 10th month was 270 days, according to the information supplied to us by the biblical verses we are investigating. We have accurately surmised, by reason of the information supplied in these biblical verses, that the months of the Noah calendar were months comprised of 30 days, and we know that the Hebrew calendar contains twelve months. It is evident that at this stage in their history, the Hebrews were using a calendar akin to that used by the ancient Egyptians whereas the year included 12 months of 30 days, making 360 days to the year, with five uncounted days, taking them to 365 days for the year. To complete the year of 360 days, from the date indicated by Genesis 8:4-5 in reference to the 10th month and 1st day, which takes us to 270 days under the Noachian chronology, we need only add the 10th, 11th, and 12th months to 270, and our year is completed at 360 days. Note Genesis 8:13: *Genesis 8:13 13And it came to pass in the six hundredth and first year, in the first month, the first day of the month, the waters were dried up from off the earth: and Noah removed the covering of the ark, and looked, and, behold, the face of the ground was dry.* This biblical passage makes clear that the Noachian Flood was completed or ended exactly one year after it began;

the series of events precipitating the flood commenced on the 600th birthday of Noah and the environment was normalized (waters dried up) on the 601st birthday of Noah – this proves beyond all reasonable doubt that the Noah Flood saga correlates to an annual solar cycle of one year, measured as 360 counted days. Of course the year contains 365 days, but five days were uncounted, according to the old Egyptian system - and I'm sure that the Hebrews were using a similar system. Actually, I believe that I see the five uncounted days within the 8th chapter, but I don't think that it's necessary that I pursue its explanation, which is very intricate, given that the data I have supplied thus far is so potent and convincing.

Review of the Noachian Saga

For the sake of clarity, I am compelled to review some of the most salient factors we have covered thus far in our investigation of the Noachian saga, beginning with the 7th chapter of Genesis*: **Genesis 7:4** ⁴For yet seven days, and I will cause it to rain upon the earth forty days and forty nights; and every living substance that I have made will I destroy from off the face of the earth.* – This chronology begins on the 1st of Tishri, the Hebrew New Years, so 7 + 40 = 47 days from the beginning of the year. They used 30-day months at this stage of their calendar's development. The rains started on the 7th day and completed after 40 days (sun's physical cosmic struggle i.e. the 40 day period of seasonal transition) on Heshvan 17, that is to say the. 2nd month, in its 17th day. The 17th day of the 2nd month is mentioned in Genesis 7:11 as the date when the 40 days of rain were completed, and the earth erupted with flooding waters from the deep, as the Bible puts it.

Genesis 7:6 ⁶*And Noah was six hundred years old when the flood of waters was upon the earth.* – Noah at 600 years is not significant to our present focus, rather the primary indicator here is that his birthday marks the first day of the year. This is made plain when in Genesis 8:13, it is stated that the earth was dried in the 601st year, 1st month, and 1st day of the month, so clearly Noah is indicated as a calendar or chronological chart of some sort, because his birthday is used to measure a cycle of one solar year. The point that we need to focus on is that Noah's birthday and the commencement of the Flood cycle are synonymous, that is to say, the first day of the month of Tishri (or its equivalent) and the anniversary of Noah's birth are the same date; therefore with this association, we are able to measure time forward with Noah's age as the yardstick, and possibly the age of Noah is a reference to the age of the chronological system that was then in vogue among the Hebrews. It states in Genesis 7:11 – that in the 600th year and second month and 17th day, the waters of the deep erupted. In Genesis 8:13, it states that in the 601st year, 1st month, and 1st day of the month, the earth was dried, so clearly they were measuring time by a chronological system designated as Noah, not an actual person named Noah that lived over 900 years; but rather a system of chronology that was, perhaps, used for a period of 900 years.

Genesis 7:24 ^{24}And the waters prevailed upon the earth an hundred and fifty days. **Genesis 8:4**^{4}And the ark rested in the seventh month, on the seventeenth day of the month, upon the mountains of Ararat. - The period of 150 days is 5 months at 30 days each; this is the period of the sun in darkness or weakness under the flood of darkness in the cosmic underworld. **The 7th month and 17th day of the month is the first Full Moon of spring**; the mountain is the mount of the vernal equinox, where the sun has mounted above the depths of the cosmic underworld. This is the same as the resurrection of Jesus on Nisan 17, and the liberation of Israel from Egypt on Nisan 17 – it is all the same symbolism, of the sun conquering and breaking free from the chains of the celestial underworld, as it ascends from the depths of the cosmic sea that lies beneath the equinoxes. The 17th of the Seventh month refers to the Jewish festival of Bikkurim or First Fruits, allegedly initiated or formalized after their liberation from Egypt – and it is likewise on the 17th that Jesus, the First Fruits, was offered or sacrificed or resurrected unto god. The underlying realty of all three symbols (Noachian, Hebrew, Jesus) is the same, that is the liberation or resurrection of the sun from beneath the equinoxes, and the birth of Spring signaled by the sun rising from the Southern Hemisphere of winter into the Northern Hemisphere of summer. All three allegories hover around the same festival, Bikkurim which is celebrated at the first Full Moon after the sun crosses the vernal equinox, not by coincidence but rather because they all signify the same underlying reality, of the emergence of the sun from the death of the cave or grave as symbolized by Jesus, or from enslavement and persecution as symbolized by Israel, or from drowning and flooding waters as symbolized by Noah.

Genesis 8:5 [5]And the waters decreased continually until the tenth month: in the tenth month, on the first day of the month, were the tops of the mountains seen. – The 10th month indicates the Summer Solstice. The New Moon signals the first day of the month, when reckoning time by the observation of the moon; even so, they were counting 30 days to the lunar month in this evolving phase of the timekeeping. This tenth month, of course, is equivalent to the month of Tammuz in the Hebrew calendar. The first day of the tenth month indicates that the sun has completed three-quarters of its annual journey, and since the Noachian year commenced at the autumnal Equinox, three-quarters of the year must indicate the Summer Solstice.

Genesis8:13[13]And it came to pass in the six hundredth and first year, in the first month, the first day of the month, the waters were dried up from off the earth: and Noah removed the covering of the ark, and looked, and, behold, the face of the ground was dry. This verse indicates that the sun's yearly circuit was completed, and they had arrived back at the 1st month and the 1st day of the month, and were in the 601st year of Noah's life, proving that a one-year cycle had been measured; the year measured out at 360 days, that was 12 30-day months. This clearly shows that the purpose of the Noah symbolism was to measure the annual solar cycle, with emphasis on the period of tribulation, the period of tribulation being the span of one hundred and fifty days when the sun is least effective in warming the earth and stimulating the atmosphere and soil. The Noah symbolism preceded the era of the mythical Moses; therefore some of the agricultural allegories that were later codified under the Mosaic mythology were not included in the Noachian mythology; those allegories not included were Passover (Pesach), Feast Of Unleavened Bread (Hag Hamatzah), Pentecost (Shavuot), The Atonement (Yom Kippur), and Tabernacles (Sukkoth). The dates of the New Years (Rosh Hashanah, 1st month, 1st day) proximate to the Autumnal Equinox, and First Fruits (Bikkurim, 7th month, 17th day) proximate to the Vernal Equinox were clearly identified. The equinoxes are the bases of the cosmic symbolism and, of course, preceded the agricultural symbolism, which is most clearly identified in the Seven Jewish Feasts. We can see that after the agricultural symbolism evolved, the Autumnal Equinox observance (however named) of Noah was merged into the Hebrew New Year (Tishri 1, Rosh Hashanah) of Moses, and the Vernal Equinox observance of Noah was blended with the Pesach, Hag Hamatzah, and Bikkurim festivals, that mark Spring amongst the Hebrews. It is also evident that the calendar, known as Noah, counted the months at 30 days each, completing the year at 360 days; later the Mosaic system evolved, which measured the Lunar Year by alternating between 29 and 30-day lunar months, making a year of 354 days, which, of course, is reconciled to the solar year by use of the Metonic cycle.

The purpose of the Noah symbolism was clearly to measure the solar year, at 360 days according to their reckoning. Ancient Egypt counted the year at 360 days and included five uncounted days to round out the year at 365 days, so it is evident that the Hebrews were using a like system, initially, in the development of their calendar. The Noah allegory contains other symbolism also, but it would detract from our focus to explore it; we are mainly concerned with proving that the bases of the myth is consistent with a focus on time keeping, and has no authentic historical bases whatsoever, not even in regards to popular flood legends. This myth is pure astronomical symbolism and completely non-historical. In regards to the plethora of Flood Legends across many ancient cultures historically, there are other cosmic cycles and/or environmental fluctuations that help explain these, and we will explain those ominous cycles later in the book.

Significance of 150 days of peril

I would like to reemphasize my assertion that the Flood of Noah was simply a means of noting the period of the sun's weakness during the winter months and the perilous affect this had on the populace: **The period of the floods worst devastation was indicated as spanning 150 days;** this number is key to recognizing the focus of the symbolism; it covers 5 months at 30 days to the month. So we should note that when we come across this number in the scriptures, whether stated as 150 days or 5 months, it is probably referring to the period of earthly tribulation (environmental adversity) that accompanied the sun's descent to lower declinations during the winter months. As I have explained previously in my other books, concerning the symbolism of the number 40: the first struggle that the sun encounters, after falling below the autumnal equinox, is the struggle of transition from summer to winter. We do not go from one season into the next instantly, but rather through a period of transition; the Ancients observed that the period of transition lasted 40 days, and they wrote this in their mythology. The moribund festival of Halloween marks the end of the 40-day period, from the Autumnal Equinox of September 22 in our modern calendars; *and then from Halloween to the Vernal Equinox (the mount Ararat) is a little less than 150 days* – this is the period of time indicated by the Noah saga, that the waters prevailed upon the earth. The actual days spanned from Halloween to the astronomical coordinate designating the Vernal Equinox (March 21) is actually about 140 days; **however**, the Ancients *measured time by the phases of the moon*, most notably the New Moon or the Full Moon; consequently they noted **the first Full Moon, after the crossing of the Vernal Equinox,** as their time indicator, and this **took them to exactly 150 days**, as measured by the date (17th of the month) of their calendar; so from the 17th of the 2nd month to the 17th of the 7th month was exactly 150 days; **this span of 150 days signifies the worst, most oppressive periods of the winter season.** The transition from summer to winter was completed by the 17th day of the 2nd month; this date marked the commencement of the period when the deleterious effects of winter were at their maximum, hence the Ancients labeled those 150 days as a time of intense torment. The 17th day of the 7th month marked the sun's crossing of the Vernal Equinox, where the sun lifted into the upper hemisphere, forecasting with its rise, warm weather, blossoming meadows, blooming trees, and burgeoning fields of grain that promised sustenance for the beleaguered survivors of the perils of winter.

Let me augment my contention concerning the true symbolic significance of the biblical references to 150 days of peril, or tribulation, as found in the Noachian saga and elsewhere in the Bible: take note of the following from Revelation of the Bible: *Revelation 9:5 through Revelation 9:6 [5]And to them it was given that they should not kill them, but that they should be tormented five months: and their torment was as the torment of a scorpion, when he striketh a man. [6]And in those days shall men seek death, and shall not find it; and shall desire to die, and death shall flee from them.* The torment described in Revelation parallels the torment of the Noah Flood (the tormenting winter endured by the Ancients); the sting of the scorpion that was associated with the torment refers, of course, to the constellation Scorpio, which was the ancient celestial indicator of winter (for the era indicated), being the first sign in the complete grips of Satan (winter). Scorpio follows Libra; Libra marks the division between the cosmic Upperworld and cosmic Underworld, but when the sun enters Scorpio, the sting of winter has arrived. The period of five months noted in Revelation is synonymous to the one hundred and fifty days noted in Genesis. This, the five months of the sun's descent into the infernal regions, was the period of great tribulation noted by the Noah symbolism as well as this symbolism in Revelation. In fact, if you

Lifting The Gnostic Veil

strip away all the nonsensical jargon of the tale, about corralling into the Ark all of the world's creatures, so as to preserve them from the flood, you will note that the main import of the saga is to instruct people to store up provisions for a long (5 months) winter. The true dynamic within all mythology is instruction; mythology was the primary means used by the Ancients to preserve their knowledge and history. For many thousands of years, ancient mankind did not possess the means or resources to pass on knowledge in books, journals or scrolls; they had to instruct their societies orally; they discovered that the use of pictures, folk tales, symbolic stories (myths), songs, dances and gestures was the most efficacious system by which to preserve their history.

The Perils of Judgment Day

The promised Judgment day is, of course, a complete and utter fabrication. We need not worry about being punished for our sins, unless society or retributive consequences take vengeance upon us. Likewise we need not anticipate equitable rewards for our charitable deeds from some imagined deity - if blessings come, they will be rendered by society in whole or in part, or by beneficent consequences sometimes justly reciprocated under the laws of cause and effect. We, of course, may feel inwardly rewarded by the doing of what we perceive as good. The so-called godly judgments of the past are all mythical, and all projections of future godly interventions are also mythical according to the best evidence – which is no evidence. Some or I could say many of our religious symbolisms concerning an alleged Day of Judgment are derived from our cultural traditions, or at least strongly influenced by them. The fundamental reasoning underpinning the concept of Judgment Day is the belief that when god finally enforces his rule upon mankind – he shall separate the wayward from the good, and destroy those that have not followed his (god's) path – whatever path that is. Supposedly the reward for those who accept god is everlasting life, while the punishment for those that reject god is everlasting death or eternal damnation i.e. death that has no end to its suffering. See the following quotes from my book The Astrological Foundation Of The Christ Myth, Book Four: *"We must constantly remind ourselves that the underlying purpose of biblical scriptures is the tracking of time – if we keep this point in mind, we are able to make practical sense out of the parallels that the biblical editors have drawn between mundane agricultural activities and the final judgment of the world. The end of the world that's referred to in much of Revelations is actually the end (the harvest) of the crop season. That may be hard to swallow but that is the bitter truth. ... The book (Revelations) is so puzzling to most that it has spawned the most insane, inane, fantastic and delusional speculations capable of being conjured up by the human mind, ..."* As we noted above, the main theme involving god's so-called Judgment of humanity is the separation of the evil from the righteous, and the subsequent destruction of those that are evil. This fanciful scenario, of *punish and reward,* is traceable, *in part,* to customs prevalent among the Ancients in anticipation of and in preparation for the oppressive winter seasons.

We need to understand clearly our options when trying to access the origins of our religious creeds – they have either sprung from the mouth of god or the mind of man. These are our only two options, and if the latter holds true, which it does, that our religious traditions originated from our own expansive imaginations, then the course to their (our religious traditions) correct evaluation is relatively simple: we need only to trace and decipher our cultural history. The correct answers to all of our religious questions, relative to the generation of the various religious creeds that we revere, lies in the records of history; but the major problem that confronts us is the monumental task of separating myth from actual history, and then accurately interpreting both the chronicles of past historical ages and the ubiquitous fables penned as historical events. Our religious ideas and concepts have been generated by our minds' interactions with our environments, our cultures, and our experiences.

The following biblical passages, that sound so ominous at their first hearing, are actually reflective of cultural symbolisms as pertaining to the customs of many ancient tribes during periods of seasonal transitions – in particular the approach of the dreaded winter season. ***Matthew 13:47 through Matthew 13:50 -*** *[47]Again, the kingdom of heaven is like unto a net, that was cast into the sea, and gathered of every kind: [48]Which, when it was full, they drew to shore, and sat down, and gathered the good into vessels, but cast the bad away. [49]So shall it be at the end of the world: the angels shall come forth, and sever the wicked from among the just, [50]And shall cast them into the furnace of fire: there shall be wailing and gnashing of teeth.* ---------- ***Revelation 14:14 through Revelation 14:16 -*** *[14]And I looked, and behold a white cloud, and upon the cloud one sat like unto the Son of man, having on his head a golden crown, and in his hand a sharp sickle. [15]And another angel came out of the temple, crying with a loud voice to him that sat on the cloud, Thrust in thy sickle, and reap: for the time is come for thee to reap; for the harvest of the earth is ripe. [16]And he that sat on the cloud thrust in his sickle on the earth; and the earth was reaped.* ***Revelation 14:19 through Revelation 14:20 -*** *[19]And the angel thrust in his sickle into the earth, and gathered the vine of the earth, and cast it into the great winepress of the wrath of God. [20]And the winepress was trodden without the city, and blood came out of the winepress, even unto the horse bridles, by the space of a thousand and six hundred furlongs.*

In order to readily apprehend the linkage between cultural traditions and biblical symbolisms, one needs to understand that these traditions started as oral renditions, poems, songs, and fables, long before the evolution of writing techniques among the Ancients. The cultural genesis for some aspects of the Judgment or wrath of god in the last days is traceable to the agricultural mythology. Of course the fall season is the subject base that symbolizes the end times in much biblical mythology. According to religion, Judgment calls for the separation of the good people from the bad people and the destruction for those that are sinful, or have not undergone rituals that indicate submission to the one monotheistic deity.

Agriculturally when the crops are harvested it follows that the tares (bad) must be separated from the wheat (good) and the bad destroyed. This is clearly in correlation to the religious conception, and actually one of the true generators of the concept. It is not a parable to help explain judgment religiously but the rather the symbol of the wheat and tares is the actual physical reality the mythical judgment represents in terms of the separation of the good from the bad.

This same theme is also reflected in the animal husbandry, in that at the advent of Fall before the winter takes hold, it was necessary that the Ancients prune their flocks of the less desirable animals. There was limited feed to nourish the animals through the winter and also limited housing to shelter the animals during the oppressive winter season. Hence the lower grade animals were slaughtered at this time of judgment (seasonal transition) and their blood overflowed the stockyards (up to the horses bridle, so to speak) during this annual ritual of judgment of the fittest (animals). The meat was preserved to feed the populace during the winter and of course the animal hides served to produce items for the use of the community. See quote from the book *Christmas in Ritual and Tradition, Christian and Pagan*, by Clement Miles, published in 1912: *"It appears...that the Teutonic peoples had no knowledge of the solstices and equinoxes...holding their New Year's Day with its attendant festivities not at the end of December or beginning of January, but towards the middle of November* [Note that the middle of November is very close to the beginning of the 150 days of tribulation as referenced above in the Noah symbolism.]. *At that time in Central Europe the first snowfall usually occurred and the pastures were closed to the flocks. A great slaughter of cattle would then take place,* [As I indicated above, the lesser animals were slaughtered but the better quality animals were preserved and sheltered] *it being impossible to keep the beasts in stall throughout the winter, and this time of slaughter would naturally be a season of feasting and sacrifice and religious observances."* These physical realities of ancient culture served as the conceptual foundation and inspiration from which the priesthood constructed their religious mythical concepts in reference to the slaughter or *reward punishment* credo inherent with the religious concept of Judgment Day (a parallel of seasonal transition in some symbolisms), in the agricultural phase of the symbolism.

The priesthood patterned their theology after the physics of nature, i.e. in reflection of natural phenomena, environmentally and astronomically. The harvest that took place in the Fall was a pattern for the harvesting of humanity as they penned it in their mythology, which over the millennia evolved into theology. The swinging of the sharp sickle, which ripped the grain from the earth and the subsequent separating of the wheat from the chaff, was likened in their mythology to the almighty god making harvest of the peoples of the earth and rewarding the faithful and casting away the wayward into perdition. The physical basis that served as a model for the spiritual judgment scene that we all are familiar with were the actual activities attendant to the annual fall harvest, and of course carries other potent symbolical content.

Within this chapter, I have attempted to exemplify Paleo-Gnostic methodology, that is to say the system by which religious mythology is *linked* with the underlying realities that the various religious fables symbolize. The underlying realities may be cultural, astronomical, agricultural, or of varying modalities, but always instructive and virtually always related to the correct tracking of time by use of the Helek (Halakim), seconds, minutes, hours, days, weeks, months, years, and many other cycles of time including units that expand into millions of years. As I have demonstrated, the system is strictly scientific, and not mystical – the interpretations are mathematical, rational, logical, and analytically verifiable by standard empirical methods. This system of interpretation or decipherment reflects the lost Gnosis of the Ancients, and should be *properly* referred to as **Paleo-Gnosticism** so as not to be confused with traditional Gnostic philosophy.

Chapter 3

The Trinity And Christ As Defined Under
Paleo-Gnostic Symbolism

The Trinity

The trinity is part of the old wisdom; it did not commence with the advent of Christian doctrine. The trinity symbolizes the tripartite structure of the Creator and his Creation, as surmised by the Ancients. The first aspect of the trinity was the Father, the Unknowable Creator, thought to be pure spirit; the second aspect was the mother i.e. matter, and the third aspect was the son, the heir of spirit and matter, and the blending of both.

According to Plato and others, god the Father or pure spirit was the *First Cause*, that emanated this universe into physical existence. Hence we could use the phrase that god begat this universe or that this universe is the first or only begotten image or the Son of god. This universe was the spirit or will of god made material or incarnate just as Jesus was the word made flesh or incarnate, according to the bible – this is pure symbolism. As we know, the person called Jesus Christ never existed in actual history, and his allegorical life is, in fact, a symbolical rendition of solar cycles for the most part. But, under the esoteric symbolism, in relation to the nature of god - Jesus and the trinity represent more than just the sun. **The dual allegory of the trinity**, inclusive of #1 the Father (Source), the Holy Spirit (Emanation), and the Son (Macrocosm, as spirit evolved to material form); or #2 the Father (Spirit), the Mother (Matter), and the Son (Macrocosm as spirit blended to matter) **is fundamental to the ageless concepts that the Ancients held in regards to the creation and maintenance of the universe** i.e. #1 creation by emanation or #2 creation by the impregnation of Spirit into Matter. Both methods leave us with the Son, that is to say the macrocosmic universe, as the issue of god, and a blend of god's spirit and formed matter. But the first method of Emanation makes the son the direct issue and essence of god, being a materialized clone of god if you will, whereas the second method of impregnation makes the son imbued with the spirit of god, but not in himself (itself) one (of the same essence) with god.

They determined that the *First Cause* of all existence was indefinable, unknowable, and invisible (not seeable or comprehensible); and this *First Cause* was identified as god, the Creator, pure spirit, knowledge, and wisdom to a degree that the human mind could not fathom; therefore they described this, the *Creator god*, as being without a name, that his name could not be uttered or pronounced, that he could not be seen with human eyes. This was their picturesque way of saying that the original *Creator god* of this universe was beyond human understanding. A name is an appellation that indicates identity and specific designation to an entity, so their saying that the *Creator god* had no pronounceable name was synonymous to saying that they could not define him. So this *unseen* and *unknowable* god became the god of gods in the theologies of the Ancients, a god that may not have been worshipped directly, but rather felt in the heart or imagined in the mind.

The lesser gods of matter (Idols) or conceptualized spirits, were imaged and idolized in accordance with the best and highest concepts that man could imagine, and worshipped accordingly. They determined that the god of gods was of such purity and divinity that any form of contact with man (matter) would be an unallowable defilement of this incomprehensible deity. Mankind required a mediator or intercessor as an avenue to the worship of the ineffable god. They determined that the ineffable god was the creator of all, and was itself, pure spirit, undefiled by matter; and that the universe was an emanation from the mind (Essence) of god, created by his Will, his Word, his Thought. They surmised that the creation of the universe was the result of the ineffable god clothing his thoughts in the form of matter, by his Will and Command. Some of them said that the world actually existed in the Mind of the Ineffable god and was therefore sustained by the Mind of the *unknowable god*. The *Creator god* is the first person of the trinity; he is the Father, and the Father is synonymous to the *First Cause* – a force that is beyond the scope of human logic to properly define.

Cosmic symbolism of Jesus Christ

All life is cause and effect; every action that takes place is the result of some stimulus or stimuli; nothing just happens without a cause or causes. Every effect was preceded by a cause, and that cause was once an effect that was preceded by another cause. When this process of cause and effect is retraced through the infinite past, we arrive at the first cause of all, and the *First Cause* of all was labeled by the Ancients as the unknowable god, the Father and Creator

The second or to put it more accurately, the third person of the trinity, i.e. the son, represents an emanation of the Father. The *First Born* (First Creation) that the Father emanated was the universe itself, as determined by the sages of old. They looked upon the *Living* universe as a creation spawned by the mind, *word* or will of god. All life proceeded forth from him and existed as spirit, as formless word or thought or wisdom or will in his mind before being made manifest in matter as matter. In their view, the whole universe contained the spirit (soul) of god and was sustained by this spirit. They saw the *Living Universe* as the instrument of god, the law of god, the image of god, and lord. They saw the *living universe* as the emanation (begotten son) of god, that ruled and punished by divine sanction.

Jesus Christ, as the incorruptible lord, is in accordance with the symbolism of nature as incorruptible, in that nature has no volition. Nature cannot sin, so to speak, because it has no will of its own, only the god ordained spirit (soul) that drives it. Jesus was a symbol of the cosmos (macrocosm), programmed nature, and as such was incorruptible –

because nature is a blind god, so to speak, without a will of its own. The universe is incorruptible, meaning it cannot sin (err, deviate) because the universe does not have a will of its own - it lacks volition. **The universe is a machine**, incapable of altering any of god's commands, but the universe is also lord and commander of all. Everything is subject to the laws of nature (symbolized by Jesus Christ) hence the universe/nature is lord and ruler. But the universe is not *the* god, as some may believe; but rather lord and ruler – the First Cause (god) is unknowable. The First Cause was perceived as non-matter, of a completely vacuous nature, devoid of all material substance, without limits (dimensions), without beginning or end, timeless. The state of *immaterial being*, which is god, cannot be measured within parameters defined by the laws of matter - all of which is incomprehensible to us. God (as surmised by the Ancients) sent (emanated) his son (macrocosm) to rule i.e. *universal nature* as lord and master. The fact that most Christians have forgotten that *God The Father* exists and choose to heap all their praises upon the son (Jesus) as lord is correct theology, according to the ancient symbolism.

The Ancients determined that we are not capable of comprehending the *Creator God*. God has no beginning or end, no form, is unlimited in scope, has no past, present or future but is a *state of being* that comprises the past, present, and future in unison - this means that god is timelessness; this, we can say or write, but cannot really understand, logically. None of us can comprehend timelessness, and incorporeally based intelligence. None of us can conceive of a god that is eternal and *never was not*. God cannot have a beginning, if so he could not be god but rather that which came before him, when he did not exist, would be god. So *god (the creator) and the lord (the ruler) are not the same*, according to the correct understanding of the ancient wisdom. God is the Creator, unseen and unknowable; but the master that governs us is the macrocosm – the *natural universe* is the true lord and master, symbolized by Jesus Christ.

The Trinity And Christ

Lifting The Gnostic Veil

Differentiation between Lord and God

We, all of us, live and die under the reign of nature - this is undeniably true. The son (lord) is the essence of the Father (god) and has always existed with (within) the Father. The spiritual or prototype universe being made or manifested as *living matter* was synonymous to the word (Christ) being made flesh. The universe has always existed within god, according to the gnosis. A good analogy is the seed or the egg which contains the essence of a tree or plant or insect or whatever within its being, unseen, concealed, latent and dormant but capable of manifestation on *command* of environmental stimuli.

The *Creator God* is the First aspect of the Trinity; he is the unknowable Father. We cannot approach the Creator God directly, if at all. Our path to god is through his son; **John 3:35 through John 3:36** *[35]The Father loveth the Son, and hath **given all things into his hand**. [36]He that believeth on the Son hath everlasting life: and he that believeth not the Son shall not see life; but the wrath of god abideth on him.*

The son is the second aspect of the ancient Trinity; the son is lord and Master. God and lord are not the same within the symbolism; each represents a different aspect of the Trinity. God refers to the unknowable Creator, and the term *lord* designates the material manifestation of the Word or Wisdom of god i.e. the Macrocosm. Matter is created and shaped by the unknowable god and also imbedded with the spirit of the unknowable god. We are governed by the lord of matter anointed with spirit i.e. we are governed by nature, which can otherwise be described as the living *Functioning Universal Order*. Nature is the inherent law by which all matter is governed. Lord means ruler, governor and supervisor; our lord is nature itself; the macrocosm is lord. Nature and the Macrocosm are synonymous. This defines the symbolism of Jesus as lord and Master, and intercessor between god and Man. Jesus, the man, never existed but his symbolism is as old as the wisdom of the Ancients. Nature is god's word made flesh (matter); our only *rational* pathway to the Creator is through the study of his Creation; this study (of nature) will bring us into a higher awareness of the unknowable Creator. See following verses whereas Jesus refers to himself (Jesus symbolizes *anointed* matter, nature) as the mirror of the unseen god: **John 8:19**[19]*Then said they unto him, Where is thy Father? Jesus answered, Ye neither know me, nor my Father: if ye had known me, ye should have known my Father also.*

Some (Pantheists) view the universe itself as the ultimate and highest god, but this cannot be true, because the universe lacks volition; the universe does not think, it acts blindly without contemplation – it is clearly a machine, an automaton, so to speak; it is capable of governance and re-creation (reproduction), however it is not the *First Cause*. The creator of the universe is the *First Cause*, i.e. the unknowable God, whose name is ineffable because he cannot be defined by logic predicated on the laws of matter. Nature is a well-tuned machine that requires balance and harmony between all of its connected parts. The imbalance of any constituent element within its wider framework could disrupt the ecology of the whole unit of which it is a part. Nature does not think; it performs only in accordance with its programming; it cannot do anything that is not written into its code, so to speak. Hence the universe cannot be the ultimate god because the universe does not possess freewill. So unless we are willing to accept god as a *non-thinking* entity, the universe cannot be god.

The harmony of the universe, incomprehensible in size, is so exact that the movement of cycles, spanning unlimited years, are measurable to the second in accuracy. This phenomenal precision indicates a force of law inherent to nature of unfathomable magnitude, a force stretching into infinity, millions and billions of light years without limits, evolving, expanding – this force is god, or the spirit of god. We cannot explain this force, therefore we cannot name this force definitively; we can only label this penetrating force as the soul or spirit of god. The Ancients called this force the soul of god, also the omnipresent spirit of god.

The Trinity And Christ

Lifting The Gnostic Veil

The notion that the universe has always existed is incomprehensible to the human mind. It is also incomprehensible that there was a time when the universe was created out of nothing. All this implies the existence of intelligence beyond our comprehension, an intelligence not governed by the laws of matter – such intelligence is defined as god. I must repeat, as was well stipulated by Maimonides others before him– we must not view the Creator god in any manner that inputs limits upon the divine; hence the supreme deity cannot be rightfully conceived as an individual entity, because such would impose limits upon the Divine, and that is not acceptable. According to the bible, god (as postulated by the biblical editors, of course) defines himself as I Am That I Am - ***Exodus 3:14*** [14]And god said unto Moses, I AM THAT I AM: and he said, Thus shalt thou say unto the children of Israel, I AM hath sent me unto you. – According to Strong's Concordance of the bible, this phrase "I Am That I Am" indicates a State Of Becoming and Existence. In consequence of this verse and other factors, we suggest that god should be considered as an All-Encompassing State Of Being, ever expanding and enveloping, but not as a nameable individual entity. We should constantly remind ourselves that the Ancients concluded that it was impossible to accurately define the Creator god, hence they stated that his name was ineffable.

Of course, the Trinity cannot be restricted to one symbolical representation. There are several astronomical versions of the Trinity represented under various symbolisms, some of which I covered in my series of books titled "The Astrological Foundation Of The Christ Myth". One explanation that we have rendered above shows the Trinity as the *Father (spirit), the Mother (matter) and Son (spirit blended to matter).* In other symbolism, the trinity is accomplished by the Father emanating his essence androgynously, so that it becomes material with his directive spirit innate to it – or, as previously indicated, in some writings he implants his spirit into existent matter (mother) so that his son (spirit blended with matter) is brought forth. The difference between the two concepts may be expressed in the philosophical differences between Monism and Dualism – whereas under monism, there is the belief that all reality, both matter and spirit is of the same essence fundamentally, derived or evolved from a common origin. Under dualism, there is the belief that spirit and matter are derived from distinct origins, hence the spark of life is caused and maintained by the interplay between opposing polarities – eternally. We can find both symbolisms within Christian doctrine, that is to say monism as expressed through Emanationism, exemplified by the word becoming flesh, reference John: Chapter One of the bible; or dualism whereas the spirit from another realm descends into matter, thereby impregnating it - reference the immaculate conception of Mary, the mother of Jesus, and other mothers of demigods referenced in ancient mythology. The symbolism of the child (son) of god with an earthly mother goes far back, in various cultures – Jesus was not the first demigod. In fact, we all are of the same blend; we all are sons of god in the spirit, according to the bible. *Romans 8:14* [14]For as many as are led by the Spirit of god, they are the sons of god. The Ancients believed that the spirit of god was embedded in all of his creation, even inanimate objects, because in order for anything to *be* (exist), whether biological or mineral, it needs direction (spirit) to form it. A stone cannot be a stone without the directive soul of god imbedded within it to form it, likewise with anything and everything – all that exist must contain the instructive soul of god (or nature if you like) in order to be whatever it is.

Freewill Or Morality Verses Instinctive Nature

We need also, to parallel the bifurcated nature of man with the theological concepts of spirit and matter, and how this nature is positively or negatively impacted culturally by these religious influences. Man is indubitably animal endowed with intelligent spirit, whether one may believe the spirit is innate, as I do, or a spark of the divine lodged within man, as some others perceive. **Metaphysically paralleled**, that is in terms of the human psyche, spirit is synonymous to freewill, and matter is

The Trinity And Christ

Lifting The Gnostic Veil

synonymous to instinctive nature. Consequently the natural moral struggle within the human species is the struggle between godly spirit (freewill or cultural morality) and satanic matter (programmed or natural instinct). And to what end is this struggle of spirit and matter fought? Is it for eventual heavenly rewards and salvation for the conquering spirits, as the Gnostics and religionists claim? Or could it be simply that a moral society is a more productive, stable and successful society, hence more efficient and thereby more conducive to the survival of the human species?

Matter is the opponent and the jailer of the spirit, according to the Gnostics. Biblically, Adam represents matter and Jesus represents spirit – 1st Corinthians 15:22 - *For as in Adam all die, even so in Christ shall all be made alive.* Allegorically, Egypt was matter and Israel (as slaves) was the spirit seeking to free itself from matter. **In regards to the human animal, pregnant with the spirit of god,** Israel/Jesus symbolizes freewill and Intelligence which represents god's spiritual presence in man, that fights to overcome the pull of the devil i.e. instinctive animal matter. In this phase of the symbolism, the bondage of Israel in Egypt under the Pharaoh represents the bondage of the Fallen godly Spirits that are imprisoned in matter, and are fighting to free themselves and return to the abodes of heaven, to god, according to the Gnostics. This parallels the Eastern theologies whereas the wayward spirits, that were once joined with god in heaven, are forced into cycles of reincarnation, as punishment and a means of purging or purification, that will earn them reentry into the abode of the spirits, according to the proponents of this concept.

Instinctive nature does not possess the capacities of love, compassion, or moral value but freewill is certainly in possession of these traits. The spirit of freewill stands in opposition to the *mechanical nature* of instinctive matter and is at war against matter (that is the instinctive animal nature of man) to guide human beings as moral imaginative creatures rather than as base programmed creatures, motivated by primal animal instincts. The lord of matter (Satan) rules this material universe but freewill and intelligence is in rebellion against instinctive nature which is the lord of this world. See bible verse: *2 Corinthians 4:4* ⁴In whom the god of this world hath blinded the minds of them which believe not, lest the light of the glorious gospel of Christ, who is the image of god, should shine unto them. This verse from 2nd Corinthians is referring, esoterically, to matter as the ruler of this world (though the Christians think the referral is to demonic spirits) and Jesus Christ parallels the *Intelligent freewill* (i.e. god's spirit, the Micro-spirit) in man that stands in rebellion to amoral, blind nature.

I need to interject at this point, that in this phase of the allegory, whereas the ruler of matter (nature) is designated as Satan; this Satan does not represent evil, but rather indicates opposition. Evil is a cultural concept, not recognized by nature. Under the trinitarian concept, as explained above, nature is embedded with the soul of god, and this is always true. God is inherently dualistic as a concept, as all existence is – we can't conceive of a front without a back, hence we need at lest two dimensions to picture anything. In order to properly envision god, we must view him through opposing prisms. The lord of matter is blind, uncompromising, unremitting, and heartless; this is the directive will of nature imbedded in all matter that compels it to become whatever it is becoming. However the spirit of freewill, that is the soul of man, is conscious of itself as an entity, and has the power of volition which instinctive nature does not possess. The soul or freewill is caged within matter (instinctive nature that knows only purpose) hence the soul (freewill) sits in natural conflict with the physical body. Nature (matter) does not recognize volition, it only knows purpose, blind purpose – freewill and its associated intelligence is the spark of the creator god in man that challenges *instinctive nature* (automated, programmed, inflexible purpose, devoid of thought and self consciousness). Man born in sin can only refer to *instinctive nature* because physical nature only recognizes purpose, it does not see morality. Physical nature is blind, and operates by reflex and instinct; but man's freewill has the power to police his physical unrestrained nature. So in this sense, that is in regards to freewill and Physical nature, we have dualism expressed in the blind (dark) forces of mechanical nature that cannot reason, and the light forces of spiritual freewill that reasons and judges the probable consequences of actions by physical nature and fights to control these natural instinctive impulses.

An example of the contention between the dark devil forces of physical nature and the godly spirit of freewill, within man, can be expressed by examining the unfolding of puberty in our youth. *Physical nature* (Satan, in this phase of the sociological symbolism) only knows purpose, it does not recognize morality, sin, love, or hate; it possesses no emotion, only the natural drive to perpetuate itself in all its assorted myriad sectors of being. Our daughters may reach puberty at the age of 10 or 12 or even earlier in some cases, in consequence, our children may approach us at these tender ages, in bewilderment, in fear, not understanding the flow of life emitting from their bodies. This is the force of nature (Devil matter) instructing its beings to perpetuate life; nature (Devil) cares nothing at all about the tenderness of youth, it only knows purpose. But it is the divine presence of the godly spirit within man, in the form of *freewill and intelligence*, that is the *counterforce* to the uncaring, brutal forces of mechanical nature. So in this phase of the symbolism, the physical body of man is the devil (matter) born of red earth and nurtured and sustained by red blood. See biblical quote from Romans of the New Testament: **Romans 7:21 through Romans 7:23** *[21]I find then a law, that, when I would do good, evil is present with me. [22]For I delight in the law of god after the inward man: [23]But I see another law in my members, warring against the law of my mind, and bringing me into captivity to the law of sin which is in my members.* Dualism is clearly indicated by these verses, the forces of the spirit representing god (As freewill and Intelligence) and the forces of matter (flesh) representing the Devil (the other face of god imbedded in matter, instinctive will or blind purpose).

Lifting The Gnostic Veil

Unfortunately, many people misconstrue *sins of the flesh* as pertaining to temptations of the flesh, relevant to sex, which is off the mark. The true import of the message stresses the eternal conflict between matter and spirit, more correctly termed *blind instinct (matter)* verses *Intelligent freewill (spirit)*. Nature does not possess freewill; it knows not right or wrong, or good verses bad; these are cultural concepts, not natural concepts. Nature is blind and bound by the laws of matter (Devil); this includes all matter, not just the sexual flesh. And as the biblical verses above indicate, the *freewill spirit* is governed by a different set of laws, that are *imaginative* and in rebellion or opposition to the laws of matter.

Freewill and Intelligence is the spark (spirit) of god in man, with cognizance of itself as an individual of importance with purpose. The human animal thinks of himself as a higher spiritual being. He holds awareness of his mortality, understands love, compassion, morality, and above all has imagination – an imagination that flies him beyond the limits of his terrestrial environment. The struggle between god and the devil therefore is the internal psychic contention of *freewill and intelligence* to withstand (resist) the temptations (instinctive impulses) of matter i.e. blind programmed natural instincts that know only purpose, *survival*. The religionists believe that when the spirit in man is victorious in this battle against Satan (matter), that he will be rewarded with spiritual immortality and not suffer the consequences of physical mortality that is predestined for all matter. At this point in their beliefs, the religionists enter into a dreamland and conjure up fantastic stories of utopian paradises (heavens) that await those freed spirits that have successfully resisted the wiles of Satan. Some claim that the reward for those who are successful, in the battles of *morality over instincts*, is liberation from the possibly endless cycles of trials (imprisonments in matter) and reincarnations of the spirit into various forms, in an effort to purge those wayward spirits. They claim that the ultimate goal of this enigmatic, continuing scenario, that we call life, is the purification of the human spirit. **And why must the human spirit be**

purified, I ask – *they say* that purification is required so that the spirit may qualify for divine rewards in a heaven or paradise that is free of the natural challenges that we experience while alive here on earth, that the final reward, for the faithful that overcome, is *rest* in the utopian splendor of god - with god.

Actually when we look deeply into the underlying psychology of this religious concept (a concept that stipulates heavenly rewards for earthly sufferings, when faith is maintained) that promises utopian rewards for the longsuffering, penitent, and faithful, we denote a primitive concept, born from cultural exigencies pressed on spiritual leaders, whose constituent populations lived lives of perpetual drudgery and toil, with little or no hope of amelioration. We can see a reflection of human realities, realities reflective of the oppressive human toils that are embodied in mankind's endless, recurring strife with his natural environment. The ultimate desire of man, locked in this incessant battle to survive against the hostile vicissitudes of nature, is rest, freedom from toil. This desire for rest was certainly more pronounced for our progenitors that lived lives much more challenging than we in these modern times. I think that it is not the least bit peculiar that the religious concepts spawned by those suffering cultures of the distant past, promised utopian bliss and rest for the faithful.

Under the paradigm of Spirits based on Physics, I can find no evidence that supports the religious concept of utopian peace as a reward for good behavior, so to speak. We can be sure that this concept was formulated, to a significant degree, in response to the anguish and misery of primitive man, warring against the odds, to survive the recurring and seemingly unrelenting onslaughts of nature (the devil). Also man's cognizance of his own mortality and the dread of this inevitable fate must have weighed heavily as a factor inducing mankind to believe in or wish and pray for some type of personal existence beyond the bonds of decaying matter.

Lifting The Gnostic Veil

Benefits of morality and social organization

The true reward for human morality is a more ordered society; human morality is the springboard to human justice. The protocols, by which we live, in large part, dictate the probable consequences of our endeavors, good or bad; it is a matter of cause and effect. Of course life has its anomalies whereas results are sometimes contrary to projected possibilities or expectations. But the results, whether positive or negative, or somewhere in between, are always definable and explainable, within the realm of human logic and experience. Man is a social animal and can only survive through cooperative efforts; hence the effectiveness of mankind's pursuits is innately tied to the quality of his social organization. The same holds true for our quality of life, whether we are safe and secure, or filled with dread and suspicion – all is inextricably tied to the modalities by which we govern ourselves. The primal instinct in man is an animal instinct, a devil instinct (devil defined as matter, instinctive blind nature) that seeks only to perpetuate itself, with total disregard for other life. If god had not instilled within man *intelligence and freewill* to counteract his base biological instincts, the strife and chaos of the animal in man would doom us to eternal turmoil and disarray - progressive civilization would be impossible. The net result of a *more ordered society* is stability, and from a base of stable governance we may acquire and preserve resources, and this accumulation of resources at some point translates into wealth, whereas the abundance of our resources mitigates against the toil and drudgery normally associated with their attainment. And when finally the mind is freed from the preoccupation and stress of wrestling against the incessantly oppressive forces of nature (Devil), it, the mind, will inevitably strive toward higher awareness in things spiritual - or some weak (less efficient) minds my lapse into hedonism, but we are focusing on the positive in this thesis. God's greatest gift to man, in my opinion, is the gift of imagination and curiosity; these traits energize man and fuel his search for answers, explanations of his being, this universe and the creator of it

The Trinity And Christ
87

all. So long as mankind is locked in hand to hand combat with nature (the devil) in the battle to survive, he is not able to focus his mind on the higher spiritual things; but the *freewill and intelligence* bestowed on man by god is the tempered knife that enables him to cut away the binds of nature, and free the mind to explore god and self. The quest for higher awareness then becomes conscious, natural and scientific, philosophical - a human quest of the human spirit, conqueror or warden of the devil (natural environment) and aspirant toward higher awareness of god through study, meditation, experience, right thinking, and divine inspiration. But the promise of spiritual liberty and enlightenment that awaits the liberated soul *is not restricted to the metaphysical world of incorporeal spirits and angels*, but rather is attainable by the spirit in man, while conscious of his human individuality, is the indication.

God the Father is the *First Cause* and as such is indefinable, beyond our comprehension. We cannot perceive a beginning of time or space and neither can we perceive the intelligence responsible for the creation of the universe – so this indefinable, unperceivable intelligence is what we call god. He (the Father) is unknown and unseen and his name is unspeakable – a name brings definition to a thing so when the Ancients said he had no name that we could utter, they were indicating that the *Father god* is undefined.

Nature Of god

It is a mistake to think that every word of the Bible, Quran and Torah is potent with esoteric meaning. Some of the dogma within religious scriptures is designed to support and reinforce certain cultural and social traditions, to aid in the effective governance of the citizenry, as well as to buttress the religious concepts promoted by the priesthood. Monotheism advocates that god is a god of love and endless compassion. He is alleged to be filled with undying love for his human children, and that we are the flowers of his creation. We were taught, at the conception of Jewish style monotheism, that the whole universe revolved around the earth, that our planet was the focal point of the universe; that, not only was the sun created to warm us and provide light for us, but according to Genesis of the bible, even the stars were created for us, to beautify and light our nights. We have now grown up, scientifically and intellectually, here in this 21st century, so that we know that we are not possibly at the center of the universe, and it has yet to be logically proven that the reason for our creation was love. There is absolutely no natural evidence that supports the hypothesis that the lord of this world is motivated by love, a personal love for his human creation.

That the relationship between god and man is based on love is *central* to monotheistic dogma; it is also the Achilles' heel of their fabricated faith, as we shall prove as we proceed. This monotheistic concept of god as a loving Father spawned quite a conundrum for the priesthood, the originators of this fictionalized doctrine, because nowhere in nature do we find love as the driving force by which god's creatures interact. Nature is, and must be, reflective of god's will, it can be no other way, unless we deny that god is the creator of all. So how could a loving god create a world of strife, predatoriness and conflict, where most animals, in order to survive, *must* prey upon weaker life forms. Within the natural habitat of our planet we see god's will in force, and that will, as reflected in the instinctive interplay between god's creatures, is heartless and amoral to any non-biased eye. The will to survive, to live, to perpetuate the species is paramount in all life forms, and the only way to preserve life is to kill (consume) other life – this is the *lord's* way, that is, if we accept his creation as a bona fide reflection of his will - and how can we do otherwise.

The populace of those bygone days saw that not only was the animal world constituted on a system of brutal internecine strife, but human culture also was reflective of the same kill or be killed plight. Their daily lives were full of turmoil and strife, hunger, drought, disease, hopelessness and misery; they toiled till their feet were bloodied and hands callused trying to wrestle edible crops from the stubborn, sometimes barren, earth. They were plagued by natural disasters, by oppressive heat or unrelenting cold – conflicts with other tribes over issues small or great was not out of the norm. So how could the priesthood reconcile the harsh, vivid realities of earthly life with the proclaimed existence of a benevolent god that they claimed had fathered mankind out of love. The concept just didn't mesh with reality. The priesthood decided that they needed to shift the cause of life's suffering from the shoulders of the Creator and fix the burden instead, upon the backs of the Creation, to convince the populace that they themselves were the cause of life's dilemmas by virtue of their disobedience to god, their flirtations with Satan, and their rejection of god's offerings of eternal blessings, evinced by their Father's (Adam and Eve) Fall from Grace by his commitment of the *Original Sin*.

Birth of the Doctrine of Original Sin

The monotheistic explanation for the misery and interminable suffering of humanity is given in Genesis of the bible, as well as in other chapters. Our life's misfortunes are thereby attributed to the doctrine of Original Sin. Allegedly, we are being punished for the sins of our father (Adam), his disobedience of god in the Garden of Eden. **Genesis 3:14 through Genesis 3:19**[14] *And the LORD god said unto the serpent, Because thou hast done this, thou art cursed above all cattle, and above every beast of the field; upon thy belly shalt thou go, and dust shalt thou eat all the days of thy life:* [15] *And I will put enmity between thee and the woman, and between thy seed and her seed; it shall bruise thy head, and thou shalt bruise his heel.* [16] *Unto the woman he said, I will greatly multiply thy sorrow and thy conception; in sorrow thou shalt bring forth children; and thy desire shall be to thy husband, and he shall rule over thee.* [17] *And unto Adam he said, Because thou hast hearkened unto the voice of thy wife, and hast eaten of the tree, of which I commanded thee, saying, Thou shalt not eat of it: cursed is the ground for thy sake; in sorrow shalt thou eat of it all the days of thy life;* [18] *Thorns also and thistles shall it bring forth to thee; and thou shalt eat the herb of the field;* [19] *In the sweat of thy*

Lifting The Gnostic Veil

face shalt thou eat bread, till thou return unto the ground; for out of it wast thou taken: for dust thou art, and unto dust shalt thou return.

These verses are clearly part of a Fairy Tale, mythology, but our faith, according to the Rabbis, Ministers, and Imams, demands that we accept this jargon as actual history – I find that amazing. These verses work fine for the priesthood that wrote them, because they give a godly proclaimed explanation for human suffering, and the blame for the toil and afflictions of humankind lies squarely on the shoulders of the populace, according to these verses - not with the so-called loving god. The monotheistic theologians tell us that god created us out of love, with the promise of eternal life and blissful happiness, but because of our dreadful sin of disobedience (eating the forbidden fruit, if you will), we are condemned to eternal tribulation in this life till we die and are buried. I suspect that these biblical verses and other similar verses of the Quran were designed to give credibility to the concept of god as a loving god, forced to punish us for our transgressions, even though nature, the best and only nonbiased witness to the true character of god, does not support such a concept.

We are taught that in Adam all die, by reason of his Original Sin, but through Christ we are all granted life, that is if we accept Christ as lord. *1 Corinthians 15:22 [22]For as in Adam all die, even so in Christ shall all be made alive --- Romans 5:12[12]Wherefore, as by one man sin entered into the world, and death by sin; and so death passed upon all men, for that all have sinned: They tell us that Christ died for the sins of the world. Romans 5:17 through Romans 5:21[17]For if by one man's offence death reigned by one; much more they which receive abundance of grace and of the gift of righteousness shall reign in life by one, Jesus Christ.) [18]Therefore as by the offence of one judgment came upon all men to condemnation; even so by the righteousness of one the free gift came upon all men unto justification of life. [19]For as by one man's disobedience many were made sinners, so by the obedience of one shall many be made righteous. [20]Moreover the law entered, that the offence might abound. But where*

The Trinity And Christ
91

Lifting The Gnostic Veil

sin abounded, grace did much more abound: [21]*That as sin hath reigned unto death, even so might grace reign through righteousness unto eternal life by Jesus Christ our lord.*

In truth, the horror of human existence has not abated from Christ's time to the present, so where lay the benefits of his alleged sacrifice some 2,000 years ago – somewhere in the future? And how long is society willing to wait for the Second Coming – a hundred years, 500, 1,000, or another 2,000 years? Clearly, the world was not made better by the coming of Christ or any other so-called prophet or messenger – so where lies the logic of it all?

They teach us also that Demons and Devils are running amuck in the world, causing disease, evil actions, violence, sin and various maladies. Of course the concept of evil spirits goes back many, many years, to the times when humanity did not understand the causal effects of nature's rampages, and consequently blamed nature's destructive and punishing aberrations on evil spirits. The monotheists, to justify their claim that god is a loving god (even though the realities of life do not support such a claim), use this concept of lurking evil spirits, along with the doctrine of Original Sin. It is also claimed that god is not the Master of this world, that the devil is king; see the following verse: **2 Corinthians 4:4**[4]*In whom the god of this world hath blinded the minds of them which believe not, lest the light of the glorious gospel of Christ, who is the image of god, should shine unto them.* The true nature or character of god, according to all the natural evidence, is that of a *stern taskmaster.* This may be disheartening at the first hearing, but nevertheless this concept is factual and provable, if we accept that the universe created by god is a true reflection of the will of god. And if nature is not a true picture of god's will, a look into the mind of god, then whom does nature represent?

God and Man

God is incomprehensible, immaterial, unseen, and unknowable, according to the Ancients – he is pure incorporeal spirit. He is eternity and timelessness, omnipresent without limits or boundaries. God is the First Cause, the sustainer, the all in all. He is the past, the present and the future in unison. The preceding explanation of the nature of god is not rational by our mundane earthly standards, rather it is conceptual and spiritual (metaphysical). Rationality is based on materiality as opposed to spirituality. In other words, since we live in a regulated universe, composed of matter - rationality and logical discernment are inherent to this physical reality, which is governed within paradigms by which we can decipher and prove facts. Logic and scientific discernments are rooted in matter; and the concepts of *time and space* are rooted in matter. Time and space cannot be measured in a universe that is completely vacuous, devoid of all substance and light, endless, empty, boundless, with nothing material in it. In such a condition of *absolute* nothingness, rationality, as we perceive it, cannot be applied, because rationality, as well as Time and Space, needs matter as a reference in order to relate. The state of complete nothingness, of metaphysical vacuity, is god, if we accept the premise that our universe was created out of nothing. The state or condition that preceded the creation of the universe was god, but not god as an individual entity, but rather as a metaphysical State of Being. We can assume that god exists or created us, by using our rationality, but we cannot prove his existence. His existence is logically *implied* but not rationally provable. Spiritual concepts cannot be validated by the rules of nature (matter) because they exist outside of the jurisdiction of matter. We know that god exist, not because of any personal or knowledgeable contact with the deity (as claimed by the monotheists), but rather because his existence is *implied*. The existence of a *creator or first cause* is *implied*, as the only logical, sensible explanation for our state of being, unless we choose to believe that this universe was created absent an intelligent cause.

The Ancients concluded that the Creator god was not knowable, not definable and consequently proclaimed that his name could not be pronounced or uttered, in other words the Creator god is beyond human comprehension and understanding, but we must accept his existence as authentic because *our* existence *Implies* the existence of an intelligent Creator. Even if we accept the premise proclaimed by some factions among the Ancients, that we are not the direct creations of the ultimate unknowable god, but rather of a lower god, termed the Demiurge by some; or even if we claim that a beginning of Time or Creation does not exist; nevertheless, the force of truth remains the same – the *First Cause* is unknowable.

The Persona or Character of god

The unknowable god cannot be sectarian; he cannot belong to the Jews, Christians or Muslims, because his state of existence is beyond our comprehension, and the claims that god has communicated directly to selected individuals is not verifiable, especially since all such claimants are dead and therefore cannot be interrogated.

Concerning the nature of god: it is assumed by some, that the emotions that we possess, such as love, compassion, grief and sympathy are *reflective* of the nature of god as a loving and compassionate deity; that these laudable attributes have been copied from god's nature into our own nature. However, the best evidence is that god is *emotionless*, and that these social attributes are merely nature's way of facilitating group cooperation and cohesiveness. The best testimonial, as to god's nature, is the natural environment, because this creation reflects the will of god. Theologically, man has created a god whose character reflects his idealized conception of god, as a loving and caring father, dedicated to the welfare of his children.

The testimony propounded by nature is that god is pure intelligence, and he functions, punishes and rewards, based on the eternal paradigm of highest reward to the most efficient while the least efficient are subject to attrition. Darwin and others called this natural phenomena the law of the *Survival Of The Fittest*, and there is no better terminology that I am aware of that better describes the judgmental character of god. Mankind imagines a god that is subject to personal request, and favors, a god that punishes him when he errs and rewards him when he is pleasing. When examined psychologically as to cause and source, it is easily recognized that this idealized conception of god is, in fact, a transference or attachment of the most exemplary parental model that man could conceive, to the imagined persona of the deity. The theological depiction of the association between god and mankind, proposed by the priesthood, parallels the classical relationship between parents and their children. Man has painted a childish character picture of god that suits his wishes and desires, but is not confirmed by reality.

Humans are social animals; we cannot survive, except as social units, as families, tribes and communities. In order to mesh as thriving communities, we must have inherent within us, emotional attributes that aid in community cohesion. It is quite apparent that god or nature has ingrained such traits within our beings as are necessary for us to function effectively as social units. Love, hate, fear, compassion, trust, distrust and so forth are instinctive to the human species, because nature (god) has deemed these traits as essential to our make up, to our success as a surviving species. All of our natural god endowed community instincts, in association with our cognitive abilities, serve to bolster and enhance the fellowship that is vital to our survival as groups, and in consequence, individually. But there is no credible indication that these traits are also a part of the character of god; the natural evidence is quite to the contrary.

When we study nature, we can find no evidence, that I am aware of, which shows the influence of emotion or prayers on the natural ecology. The clarion call of nature is for the maximum efficiency of all its parts; the maxim *survival of the fittest* rings louder than any other call, and the immediate or eventual destruction of the least efficient forms within nature follows in natural consequence. All life, in order to survive, must consume other life; this is nature's (god's) way. This indicates an instinctively predatory inclination imbedded in the nature of most life forms, *as ordained by god*. Life is naturally competitive, at all levels; the most efficient and stronger forms are rewarded by nature (god) with continued life and the weaker inefficient forms are cast into the pit, so to speak.

It's very jolting and discomforting for most of us to confront the realities of the true character of god, as a dispassionate taskmaster. This goes against the prevailing attitudes of most cultures, that wish to see themselves favored in the eyes of god as most of us are favored in our own eyes. But with understanding, I think that we will discover that god's way is the best way, for us, and for all creation. As I wrote above, the character of god, as fashioned by the monotheists, follows the model of beloved parents; this is the paradigm by which they have styled their deities. But which type parent (god) is better in the long run, given the following choices: **Type A:** a parent that is reliable, trustworthy, capable, just, always the same, completely predictable, always on time, never failing in its promises, never punishes out of anger but only when you infract its commands, always warns of danger if you are wise enough to recognize the signals, promotes efficiency by rewarding it, sets no limits on our ambitions – (we must impose our own limits reflective of the environment and circumstances), gives us complete freedom to explore and investigate at will; *this is the parent called nature (reflective of god's will)*. **Type B:** a parent that is prone to anger, vacillating, sometimes responsive to prayer – sometimes not responsive, conceited and demanding of constant praise, moody, unpredictable, sometimes loving sometimes ill-tempered, burdens us with excessive rules and rituals, subject to change the rules by which we live at a whim or as a favor to some, jealous, demands sacrifices of blood and wealth, arbitrary and threatening; *this is the monotheistic deity of Judaism, Christianity, and Islam.*

The Natural Order

God (nature) demands efficiency and, in consequence, rewards efficiency when it is achieved; this is god's way and the best way, in my opinion.

Lifting The Gnostic Veil

Nature rewards efficiency, when coupled with wisdom, without fail. The response of nature is completely predictable to any set of circumstances if we have the knowledge and wisdom to correctly analyze the situation. The wealth, opulence and convenience that pervades the lives of many in this modern world, as opposed to the pervasive poverty, toil and misery of ages gone by, is clear and indisputable evidence that nature (god) rewards efficiency. Our improved efficiency, in this modern age, has produced greater economic and other associated rewards for us, without doubt. Life is cause and effect and greater efficiency produces greater more favorable effects (results) in whatever endeavors we pursue.

In accordance with god's design, we live in a world of rewards (blessings) and consequences (punishments) which are determined by our causal efforts, coupled with the applications of efficiency and wisdom, in association with good or bad fortune, which is not under our control and may, at times, help or hinder our efforts. Those who are wise, strong, and efficient thrive in a godly world of just rewards and consequences but the weak and inefficient are pulled under, in accordance with god's design. The deluded and less fortunate may, under their various religious banners, seek special favors from god through prayerful supplications, *to alter the natural courses of cause and effect*, so that they are rewarded even when reward is not justly mandated by the *natural law of cause and effect*; if god answered, or was even capable of answering such supplications, with results that run counter to the natural order of cause and effect, such would upset the harmony and balance of nature, in total. Hence godly intervention is impossible, if the requested effect runs counter to the natural cause of its generation.

Natural order is a series of causes and effects, infinitely interlinked and intertwined. God cannot alter one natural effect without wreaking devastation upon the whole interlocking system. No effect happens in isolation but rather is linked interminably through an endless maze of naturally generated consequences. Special favors from god are naturally

The Trinity And Christ
97

impossible, because god's systems of natural laws do not allow for exceptions to the natural order. If exceptions were allowed, then natural and universal order would be overturned. The god of monotheism is an imposter, based on this reality alone. Think of the ridiculous assertion made in the bible that Joshua solicited help from god to aid his battle against his enemies and the lord answered by causing the sun and the moon to halt in their courses. This, of course, means that the earth ceased to rotate on its axis, if it were true - ***Joshua 10:13[13]And the sun stood still, and the moon stayed, until the people had avenged themselves upon their enemies. Is not this written in the book of Jasher? So the sun stood still in the midst of heaven, and hasted not to go down about a whole day.*** Such favors from god are *not* possible in the real world; they only happen in the fanciful world of mythology. I cannot imagine the consequences of the earth ceasing to rotate. Think of the repercussions of such an event; but not only that, think of the repercussions attendant to god answering the prayers of those who would like him to prevent earthquakes, floods, storms, avalanches, droughts, disease, war, crime, grief and so forth. These physical and social traumas do not occur without natural or sequential causes; they are effects generated by real causal forces. To disrupt the naturally occurring effects, generated by the natural laws of cause and effect, would eradicate the effects of natural law, resulting in the implosion of the universal order. The violent outburst of our planet resulting in storms and earthquakes and the like, are generated by *real* geological and atmospheric pressures that must be released; it is not within the power of god to negate these forces without negating the natural laws by which they are generated, and if we lose natural law, we lose the equilibrium by which the universe is sustained.

The concept of a personal god, analogous to parents caring for their children, was clearly designed to instruct people whose intellect was underdeveloped and in the embryonic stages of societal development, with little scientific understanding of the natural environment. Reference this quote from the book *Moral And Dogmas* by Albert Pike, wherein he quotes a Greek philosopher of the ancient world: *"All virtue is a struggle; life is not a scene of repose; but of energetic action. Suffering is but another name for the teaching of experience, appointed by Zeus himself, the giver of all understanding, to be the parent of instruction, the schoolmaster of life. He indeed put an end to the golden age; he gave venom to serpents and predacity to wolves; he shook the honey from the leaf, and stopped the flow of wine in the rivulets; he concealed the element of fire, and made the means of life scanty and precarious. But in all this his object was beneficent; it was not to destroy life, but to improve it. It was a blessing to man, not a curse, to be sentenced to earn his bread by the sweat of his brow; for nothing great or excellent is attainable without exertion; safe and easy virtues are prized neither by gods nor men; and the parsimoniousness of nature is justified by its powerful effect in rousing the dormant faculties, and forcing on mankind the invention of useful arts by means of meditation and thought."* This says it all, or at the least holds as much significance for us in this day and time as for those of the past.

Chapter 4

The Great Cycle Of Axis Rotation

Primitive Man's impressions of his world

I cannot overstress the significance of *time tracking* as the chief and fundamental purpose of ancient mythological symbolism. Of course, it was essential that the Ancients track and calculate the seasonal cycles accurately in order to plant and harvest at the appropriate times of the year. If they failed at this task they risked famine and mass starvation. The greatest fear of ancient human societies was starvation, followed by the fear of the dreaded and oppressive winter season, and that followed by the fear of the night. In the earliest stages of human development all activity froze at the daily setting of the sun, as if locked in a vise, till the morning light returned. The primitives would huddle together in dread and fear of the night creatures and/or take to caves, and trees, and various barricades, and huts to protect themselves from the attacks of beasts that preyed under the cover of darkness. We must remember that fire was a rare and precious commodity in those early primeval days.

If we allow ourselves to connect with the probable mindset that prevailed in those bygone days, when our earliest spiritual concepts were being initially cultivated or at least the seeds of such thoughts were being psychologically imbedded – we will concurrently achieve greater awareness and intuitive abilities, that will aid us significantly in understanding and interpreting mythological symbolisms, symbolisms based to a great extent on the struggles between man and his leading environmental nemeses: hunger, disease, intense heat or cold, darkness, and the unpredictable rampages of nature. The unpredictable rampages of

Lifting The Gnostic Veil

Mother Nature were the apparently spontaneous upheavals of nature manifested in the forms of violent weather, earthquakes, floods, droughts or whatever, that ancient man generally attributed to the anger of the gods or spirits; although after many hundreds and thousands of years, man began to recognize that even the seemingly sudden and violent outbursts of nature were actually preceded by signs or indicators – indicators that the Ancients eventually evaluated, and described in their mythologies. The prime indicator of the most severe and lasting alterations in the earthly environment were changes in the inclination of the earth's axis, which man learned to track by various means, including the monitoring of changes in the Obliquity of the Ecliptic which changes in sync with the migrating axis.

Inherent Volatility of Earthly Environment

Our environment holds the potential for danger and death that goes far beyond the cognizance of most of us. I refer to the dangers embodied in the natural volatile character of our collective *mother*, this earthly planet - this erupting, unstable, evolving, dynamic *living thing*, bulging with fire and molten rocks, poison gases, Arctic winds, flooding waters, pestilence, and deadly or mutilating radioactivity. Our planet and universe are ever changing – they are not stable. Some of the changes are apparently random but others are cyclical and deadly.

The Ancients were successful in calculating some of our planet's cycles that tend to instigate adverse environmental traumas for the organisms that populate this planet, including humans, and all other animals, as well as plants, trees and what have you. Some of the symbolisms of the Ancients were actually focused on these expanded planetary cycles that span beyond the seasonal cycles, and, in some cases, even beyond the Astrological Cycles (2,160 years), and beyond the Precessional Cycles (25,920 years). The changes that occur and reoccur to our planet over millions of years are so drastic that the appellation *destruction* is justifiable but not accurate; the description *transformation* is more accurate.

Evolution

According to some that have researched these issues, the dynamical changes that afflict our planet are so pronounced that it seems that the world is destroyed and a new world is born, similar to the annual destruction of the *winter world* that initiates the *creation* (birth) of the *summer world*, and vice versa. This is because as the planet changes, all living things (organisms) that inhabit the planet must also change in order to survive – they must adapt or mutate in accordance with the demands of the evolving planetary environment. Indeed we humans are the results of evolution, each *major* racial division (African, Asian, and Caucasian), while in primeval isolated geographical pockets, evolved in adaptation to environmental stimulus, although some, according to various ancient mythologies, retrogressed and became simian, that is, in mythological vernaculars they were cursed or punished by being transformed into apes. This is expressed in the Muslim Quran: Surah 7: 166 "When in their insolence they transgressed prohibitions, we said to them, be ye apes – despised and rejected"

We are *not* the results of linear progressive evolution from so-called lower forms to higher forms, but rather our evolution has been and *is* adaptive to the ever-changing environments of our planet. All of our prominent racial characteristics were designed by god (nature) to facilitate survival in distinct climatic conditions. Traits such as wide nostrils designed by nature to intake, moisturize, and filter at appropriate ratios the hot dry air of torrid climates; or narrow nostrils designed to intake, and warm, and filter the frigid air of Arctic climates; or squinted (epicanthic fold) eyes along with longer arms and torsos, proportionately shorter legs that result in lowered centers of gravity for the human body so as to efficiently navigate in very windy climates; or kinky, wooly (head) hair, for those that dwell in extremely hot climates with little shade, designed to retain moisture (water) and utilize its cooling effects for the head that encases the brain; and black hairless skins designed to efficiently sweat and bath the body with cooling moisture, and better resist the perils of the sun's rays and absorb and disseminate its beneficial properties and/or dissipate its maleficent properties.

Likewise with all other living things, when nature detects (or we might say, when the sensors naturally innate to organisms detect) that a species cannot survive, *in a radically changing environment*, as biologically or organically constructed, it (nature) genetically reconstructs the offspring of the species (organisms), successively, through mutations, over generations, until the necessary adaptations for viability are acquired. This is witnessed currently in modern society when insects mutate in order to adapt to radically changed environments caused by insecticides or when microorganisms mutate in order to adapt to radically changed environments caused by antibiotics. The processes of natural reproduction, innate in all life forms, attendant with genetic adaptations or mutations, as signaled or instigated by our evolving and unstable environment (i.e. unstable for us over protracted aeons), assures the perpetuation of life, in its varied adaptive forms, regardless of the twists and turns of our earthly habitat.

The Unfathomable Universe

Our grand universe is limitless, but our astronomers have provided us with much data on the expansiveness of the known or *visible* universe. Our Solar System, i.e. the sun and the planets that revolve around the sun, resides in the Milky Way galaxy. The Milky Way is composed of billions of stars – some Astronomers estimate 200 billion stars. Our galaxy is 100,000 to 120,000 *light years* in diameter. Light travels at approximately 186,000 miles per second, so in one year light travels about 5.88 trillion miles. Our galaxy is just one of many galaxies – astronomers say that there are over **240 billion galaxies** in our *visible* universe!

Our sun does not just hang suspended in space, but like all other stars, our sun is cycling through space – it takes the sun about 250 million years to make a complete revolution about the hub of the Milky Way galaxy, according to the astronomers. During this journey of 250 million years the sun will take us i.e. our planet earth, and our sister planets into deep regions of space of unknown variations that may impact significantly upon our earthly environment.

Considering the vastness of the visible universe, not to mention the endless segments of the universe beyond the sights of our telescopes and calculations, I think that it is profoundly absurd to believe that we here on earth are the only living creatures in the universe; and it is even more ridiculous to believe that other intelligent beings, wherever in the universe they may reside, are worshippers of Yahweh, Jesus, or Allah. And if our earthly gods are not indeed universal gods, worshipped everywhere in the universe, of what real value is our faith? I humbly declare: if the Ancients had truly known and understood the unfathomable vastness of the universe, as we now comprehend it, they would have never dreamed up the puerile religious doctrines that we now vainly cherish.

Aspects of the Great Cycle Of Axis Rotation referenced in the Book of Enoch

Within this chapter we shall discuss those large cycles that instigate dramatic changes in our earthly environment, and climax with the grandest of the earthly cycles, which is the cycle that I call the *Great Cycle of Axis Rotation*, a cycle that spans 2,160,000 years. We shall uncover some of the obscure methods by which the Ancients tracked and recorded those large cycles. We shall explain the astronomical variations that indicate the opening and closing of various stellar cycles that serve as profound indicators of significant alterations in the earthly environment. Witness now these following passages from the Book of Enoch, that will aid in our explanations:

Book Of Enoch: Chapter 18: 14 –16: [14]And there I beheld seven stars, like great blazing mountains, and like spirits entreating me. [15]Then the angel said, This place, until the consummation of heaven and earth, will be the prison of the stars, and the host of heaven. [16]The stars which roll over fire are those which transgressed the commandment of God before their time arrived; for they came not in their proper season. Therefore was He offended with them, and bound them, until the period of the consummation of their crimes in the secret year

Book Of Enoch: Chapter 64: 1 – 4, 9 – 10: [1]In those days Noah saw that the earth became inclined, and that destruction approached. Then he lifted up his feet, and went to the ends of the earth, to the dwelling of his great-grandfather Enoch. [3]And Noah cried with a bitter voice, Hear me; hear me; hear me: three times. And he said, Tell me what is transacting upon the earth; for the earth labours, and is violently shaken. Surely I shall perish with it. [4]After this there was a great perturbation on earth, and a voice was heard from heaven. I fell down on my face, when my great-grandfather Enoch came and stood by me.

Book Of Enoch: Chapter 65: 1 – 2: [1]After this he showed me the angels of punishment, who were prepared to come, and to open all the mighty waters under the earth: [2]That they may be for judgment, and for the destruction of all those who remain and dwell upon the earth.

Book Of Enoch: Chapter 66: 3 – 7, 13 – 14: [3]The seed of life shall arise from it, and a change shall take place, that the dry land shall not be left empty. I will establish your seed before me for ever and ever, and the seed of those who dwell with you on the surface of the earth. It shall be blessed and multiplied in the presence of the earth, in the name of the Lord. [4]And they shall confine those angels who disclosed impiety. In that burning valley it is, that they shall be confined, which at first my great-grandfather Enoch showed me in the west, where there were mountains of gold and silver, of iron, of fluid metal, and of tin. [5]I beheld that valley in which there was great perturbation, and where the waters were troubled.[6]And when all this was effected, from the fluid mass of fire, and the perturbation which prevailed [(62)] in that place, there arose a strong smell of sulphur, which became mixed with the waters; and the valley of the angels, who had been guilty of seduction, burned underneath its soil. [7]Through that valley also rivers of fire were flowing, to which those angels shall be condemned, who seduced the inhabitants of the earth ....13In those days shall the waters of that valley be changed; for when the angels shall be judged, then shall the heat of those springs of water experience an alteration. [14]And when the angels shall ascend, the water of the springs shall again undergo a change, and be frozen. Then I heard holy Michael answering and saying, This judgment, with which the angels shall be judged, shall bear testimony against the kings, the princes, and those who possess the earth

Indeed the scenarios depicted in the Book of Enoch are very ominous and foreboding - the book clearly describes earthly upheavals that threaten the lives of the earth's inhabitants. Actually that which the Book of Enoch is describing is clearly an earthly upheaval, that is to say, a violent climatic and geographical restructuring of the planet, caused by the natural cyclical processes of nature – and not by an angry god, as the unenlightened and superstitious tend to believe.

A natural earthly upheaval is clearly evident by the assertions made within the book that the waters (lakes, rivers, seas, underground deposits) were expanded beyond their prior boundaries: *"open all the mighty waters under the earth", "[8]The seed of life shall arise from it, and a change shall take place, that the dry land shall not be left empty."* Also noted, are changes in the climate from Temperate zones to Arctic zones: *"13In those days shall the waters of that valley be changed; for when the angels shall be judged, then shall <u>the heat of those springs of water experience an alteration</u>. [14]And when the angels shall ascend, the water of the* *springs shall again undergo a change, and be frozen.*" Earthquakes and volcanic eruptions are indicated: "*⁶And when all this was effected, from the fluid mass of fire, and the perturbation which prevailed ⁽⁶²⁾ in that place, there arose a strong smell of sulphur, which became mixed with the waters; and the valley of the angels, who had been guilty of seduction, burned underneath its soil. ⁷Through that valley also rivers of fire were flowing*". **Above all, the indicator and forecaster of these cataclysms is identified as the changing attitude of the earth's axis:** "*: ¹In those days Noah saw that the earth became inclined, and that destruction approached.*"

It cannot be any clearer - the Ancients, as noted in the Book of Enoch have pinpointed the changing attitude of the earth's axial inclination as the harbinger or indicator of great earthly upheavals: "*¹In those days Noah saw that the* **earth** *became* **inclined, and that destruction approached**." And we assert further that the Ancients were successful in measuring the rate or cycle that governed the change of the earth's inclination, and that many of the mythological symbolisms of the monotheistic scriptures, and symbolisms of other ancient cultures were actually geared toward tracking the gradual migration of the earth's axis i.e. the Great Cycle of Axis Rotation.

Lifting The Gnostic Veil

The following graphic will help exemplify the relationship between the Pole of the Ecliptic, the earth's Celestial Pole, and the Obliquity of the Ecliptic. This is important because, above all, the changing positions in the relationship between the two Poles was the harbinger or indicator of significant changes in the earthly environment, and the Ancients were able to track the changes in the positions of the Celestial Pole by monitoring changes in the expanse of the Obliquity of the Ecliptic which changes in sync with the movement of the Celestial Pole.

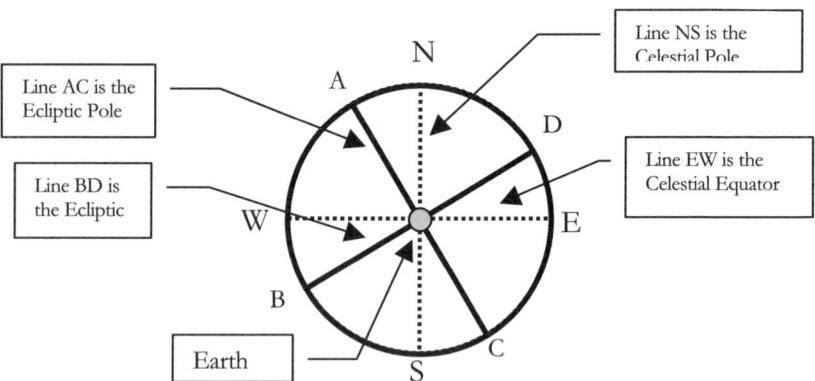

Point "N" on the chart is the earth's Celestial North Pole, and Point "A" on the Chart is the North Ecliptic Pole. The arc between NA spans 23.5 degrees. The arc ED is the expanse of the Obliquity of the Ecliptic also at 23.5 degrees. The Pole of the Earth i.e. line NS is rotating counterclockwise toward the Pole of the Ecliptic i.e. line AC at the rate of one degree every 6,000 years. As the earth's Pole (NS) rotates so does the point of the earth's equator (EW) so that Ancients were able to track the distance between the Poles, Ecliptic and Celestial, by measuring the expanse of the Obliquity of the Ecliptic (Arc ED) which is equal to the spread between the Poles (Arc NA).

The Great Cycle Of Axis Rotation

Lifting The Gnostic Veil

Tracking Changes in the Inclination of the Earth's Axis

In truth the earth is continuously transfiguring itself, climatically and geographically, over thousands and millions of years. Unfortunately many of us think that current climate conditions are the norm, but in fact the planet does not have a climatic norm over the long term – unless you want to call *change* the norm. The inhabitable regions of our planet undergo continuous transformations, variations, and *relocations* over the millennia, over many, many thousands of years. Of course, some who have studied these issues assert that some changes come quickly, and catastrophically; however I, in this essay, am focused on *measured* changes as indicated in the mythology of the Ancients. It is this measured altering of the earthly environment that I shall explain as we proceed, or more accurately I should say that I shall explain the symbolism related to this change, and some of the methods used by the Ancients in tracking time, related to the earth's axial migration.

The Ancients discovered that many of the earth's upheavals and/or drastic alterations of the climate were associated with the changing obliquity of the ecliptic, that is to say the tilt of the earth's axis to the Plane of the Ecliptic. Hence the tracking of this gradual change in the earth's axial orientation became of extreme importance – and much of the symbolism of the scriptures as well as the architecture of various temples and monuments were actually geared toward tracking the Great Cycle of Axis Rotation.

As I have already noted, the Great Cycle of Axis Rotation completes itself in the course of a cycle that spans *two million one hundred and sixty thousand years* (2,160,000 years). This is the span of time that it takes the celestial projection of the earth's axis to rotate vertically from East to North, from North to West, from West to South, and back to the East - a cycle of 360 degrees at the rate of one degree every 6,000 years.

The Great Cycle Of Axis Rotation

Lifting The Gnostic Veil

At present our earth is tilted from the *Pole of the Ecliptic* at an angle of approximately 23.5 degrees; therefore 18,000 years from now the angle will reduce to 20.5 degrees, that is a change of 1 degree of arc every 6,000 years – and of course that means that 24,000 years ago the tilt of the axis was 27.5 degrees from the Ecliptic Pole. The rate of axial rotation is measurable as .6 seconds of arc in one year, or 1 minute of arc every 100 years, 10 minutes of arc every thousand years, or 60 minutes of arc (1 degree of arc) every 6,000 years. Our planet is now inclined 23.5 degrees from the Pole of the Ecliptic, so in 141,000 years (23.5 times 6,000 = 141,000) our earth's celestial pole will be in union (angular similarity) with the Pole of the Ecliptic – and we, or I should say our descendants, will experience one season annually. It is worth noting - three thousand years ago, when much of our scriptural information was being edited and organized, and some monuments were being built, the earth's axial incline was 24 degrees and the span to union with the ecliptic's pole was 144,000 years.

Before I continue with our explanations of the Great Cycle of Axis Rotation, I should note that *modern* astronomers are aware of the fact the earth's axial orientation is not fixed. I don't think that they are aware of the implications of the ancient mythology in this regard, but nevertheless they have calculated that the earth's axis is not *fixed* to the present tilt of 23.5 degrees. They claim that the earth's axis oscillates within a range of 2 degrees in a cycle that spans 41,000 years. They call this cycle the *Milankovitch cycle*. They give various scientific and astronomical reasons for why the earth's axial orientation is not fixed, and claim that the variation is limited to a span of two degrees back and forth over forty-one thousand years. I can't imagine that academia, as a whole, will ever admit publicly, even if they are aware of it, that the axial inclination of the earth revolves 360 degrees – the religious and social consequences would most certainly be discombobulating.

The Great Cycle Of Axis Rotation

Lifting The Gnostic Veil

The natural struggles and hardships that humans must endure and overcome in order to survive under the radically altered climatic and geographical environments attendant to the earthly upheavals that must accompany the continuous change of the earth's axial incline are mind-boggling, and of course, not consistent with the monotheistic concept of a loving, doting god. Of course *we* are primarily interested in the *science* of the Ancients, and according to their science *as revealed in their mythology*, the migration of the axis is not limited but rather total and continuance at 360 degrees per cycle over 2,160,000 years.

The truth of the Ancients dictates that the changing inclination of the earth's axis is not *limited* or nearly as agreeable or non-threatening as our modern academics would like us to believe, although some modern scientist do believe that the Ice Ages are associated with the changing inclination of the earth's axis, that is, as defined by the Milankovitch Cycle. The assertions that I am offering are based solely on interpretations of ancient mythology as decoded under Paleo-Gnostic methodology, by me, and by some others who have previously written on or speculated on these matters, in fact many have *speculated* on these matters.

Implications of the changing inclination of the earth's axis

The sun is the life-giver and the governor of our planet. The lengths of our days and nights, the seasons, the climates, the volumes and boundaries of the seas, lakes, and rivers are all related to the sun (also the moon), and the dispersal of the sun's light on our planet. The dispersal of the sun's rays upon the earth is tied directly to the obliquity of the ecliptic. The Obliquity of the Ecliptic is equal to the angle of inclination of the earth's axial Pole to the Ecliptic Pole. The Obliquity of the Ecliptic is the span or distance between the sun's position at the celestial equator[8] and its

---

[8] The Celestial Equator is simply the position of the earth's equator extended into the sky above for use as a celestial coordinate

farthest point north or south of the celestial equator – this span is presently 23.5 degrees or so.

When the sun is positioned at the celestial equator, we call that position the Equinox; when the sun is positioned at 23.5 degrees north of the celestial equator, we call that position the Summer Solstice; when the sun is stationed 23.5 degrees south of the celestial equator, we call that position the Winter Solstice. Our seasons are determined by the Obliquity of the Ecliptic – summer begins when the sun is at its highest in the earthly sky, 23.5 degrees above the celestial equator at the Summer Solstice; winter begins when the sun is at its lowest point, 23.5 degrees south of the celestial equator at the Winter Solstice; and Spring or Fall begin when the sun is astride the equinox.

The extent of the Obliquity of the Ecliptic changes in sync with the inclination of the earth's axis to the plane of the ecliptic, or we could say the extent of the Obliquity of the Ecliptic changes in sync with and is equal to the change of the angle of the earth's axial Pole to the Pole of the Ecliptic. It is very easy to comprehend why the Ancients were tenaciously focused on tracking changes in the extent or range of the Obliquity of the Ecliptic which, of course, simultaneously provided correlating data on the changes in the earth's axial inclination to the Pole of the Ecliptic, in that these changes are indicative of profound environmental impacts upon our planet.

Climatic Zones and the Obliquity of the Ecliptic

The climatic zones of our planet are gauged in accordance with the extent of the Obliquity of the Ecliptic. We have three major climate zones on our planet – they are the Tropics, the Arctic, and the Temperate. The Tropic Zone is the zone defined by the oscillation of the sun between the solstices, the Tropic of Cancer measures from zero degrees latitude to 23.5 degrees *north* latitude, and the Tropic of Capricorn measures from zero degrees latitude to 23.5 degrees *south* latitude – the entire region of 47 degrees expanse is the Tropics. The Arctic Zones are the regions within 23.5 degrees of the North Pole and likewise the South Pole. The region from latitude 66.5 degrees north to 90 degrees north is defined as the Northern Arctic Region, and the region from latitude 66.5 degrees south to 90 degrees south is defined as the Southern Arctic Region. The regions that lay between 23.5 degrees north latitude and 66.5 degrees north latitude, and likewise between 23.5 degrees south latitude and 66.5 degrees south latitude are the Temperate Zones. The Temperate Zones carry the most favorable weather, not too hot and not too cold, but these zones are not constant due to the gradual changing inclination of the earth's axis over many thousands of years.

The Northern Arctic Region does not receive sunlight year around, but is subject to about six months of daytime when the earth is inclined toward the sun during the six months of the northern hemisphere's Spring and Summer; and about six months of darkness when the earth is inclined away from the sun during the Fall and Winter seasons – the Southern Arctic Region experiences the same six months of daytime and nighttime in reverse sequence. Of course, this means that as the angle between the earth's Celestial Pole and the ecliptic's Celestial Pole expands or retracts over thousands and millions of years, those geographical sections of the earth that fall within the boundaries of this change will likewise experience days and nights that run for months instead of in twenty-four hour cycles. For instance, if the tilt of the earth was at 60 degrees instead of 23.5 degrees, then fully all the area with within 60 degrees of the poles would experience days of several months duration, and nights of several months duration, as is the present case for our Arctic regions. When the planet is inclined at 90 degrees, fully half the planet will experience months of continuous daylight and months of continuous darkness.

Indications are that the other planets in our solar system, and I would assume the whole universe, undergo the same rotations of their axes. The present axial inclinations of some other planets are as follows, rounded off to the nearest degree: Mercury 0 degrees, Venus 177 degrees, Mars 25 degrees, Jupiter 3 degrees, Saturn 27 degrees, Uranus 98 degrees, Neptune 28 degrees, Pluto 120 degrees. Some planets have axes that are in retrograde motion. Axial retrograde indicates an inversion of the North Polar Axis so that the axis of a planet seems to rotate clockwise instead of counterclockwise. This occurs in inclinations between 90 degrees and 270 degrees. The result of this retrograde action is that the sun and other cosmic entities rise in the West and set in the East - the opposite of our present reality. This is a difficult concept for many to wrap their brains around, sort of like waters in the Southern Hemisphere that spiral to the left instead of to the right when going down the drain. Herodotus made mention in his Histories that the Egyptians told him that their history revealed to them that there was a time when the sun rose in the West instead of in the East. There has been and is much speculation on the Inversion Of The Poles – I am convinced, according to my understanding of the ancient mythologies, that the Ancients were studiously tracking cycles that related to the inversion of the Poles, or the gradual migration of the earth's axis toward angular union with the ecliptic axis; and their fixation on this tracking was due to the fact that they viewed the migration of the Celestial Pole as the harbinger of possibly severe environmental impacts upon our planet. I write *possibly severe*, because at some stages in the Great Cycle of Axis Rotation the migration of the Pole also indicates relief from oppressive environmental conditions.

Understanding the Precession of the Equinoxes as viewed by the Ancients

The Precession of the Equinoxes covers a span of 25,920 years, during which the position of the equinox circuits westward through all the twelve signs of the zodiac. Traditional astronomy explains this precessional phenomenon as resulting from the slow wobble of the earth as it rotates on its axis, and the gravitational pull of the sun, moon, and planets upon the earth. All these forces, and others, combined therewith cause the earth to gyrate so that the direction of its axis paints an ellipse in the heavens that cycles through the circumpolar constellations, namely Ursa Minor, Cepheus, Cygnus, Lyra, Hercules, and Draconis; and in tandem causes the position of the equinox to cycle through the twelve signs of the zodiac, which tracks the ecliptic, over a complete precessional cycle of 25,920 years or so. The scientific explanation as to why we have precession is not relevant to the ancient symbolism, only the concepts of the Ancients and their views of the phenomenon are important or relevant to interpreting the ancient symbolisms involving the migration of the celestial pole.

To the Ancients the precessional cycle was the Great Year or cycle of 25,920 years in which *the earth's Celestial Pole revolved around the Pole of the Ecliptic.* The Pole of the Ecliptic is located at Right Ascension18 hours, Declination +66.5 degrees, right in the first curl of the constellation Draconis. Draconis curls around the Pole of the Ecliptic like a serpent curling around the trunk of a tree. The Ecliptic Pole is situated in the middle, midst, or center of the circle or ellipse traced by the earth's Celestial Pole. See graphic on next picture page, and you'll notice that the earth's celestial Pole traces a circle that encloses the Pole of the Ecliptic and Draconis (the serpent). This of course represents the Precessional phase of the Garden of Eden symbolism. The *dotted* circle in the graphic shows the path of precession (the path of the earth's Celestial Pole) through the circumpolar constellations of Draconis, Ursa Minor, Cepheus, Cygnus, Lyra, and Hercules with one of its (his) feet directly above the head of Draconis.

The Great Cycle Of Axis Rotation

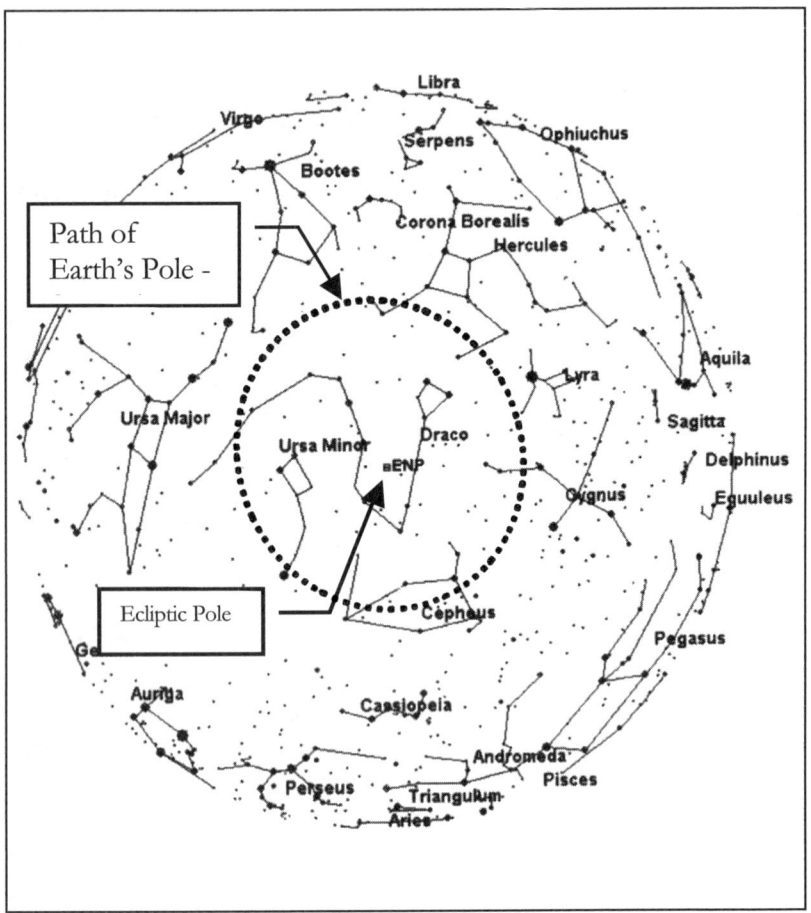

Figure 2: The dotted circle is the path of the earth's Celestial Pole over 25,920 years - one cycle of precession.

Actually the earth's Celestial Pole does not really trace a circle around the Pole of the Ecliptic, *that is from cycle to cycle*, but rather it traces a *spiral* around it. The earth's Celestial Pole has for several thousands of years been moving closer and closer to the Pole of the Ecliptic, pursuant to eventual angular similarity or union. The Ancients depicted this movement as a spiral, which indicates, that with the completion of each precessional cycle the earth's Celestial Pole is stepping four degrees or more closer to the Pole of the Ecliptic - the Pole of the Ecliptic being located at the center of the spiral. The Ancients were able to measure this movement of the Celestial Pole, (in some recent eras, as is presently, moving toward the Ecliptic Pole, or in some distant eras moving away from the Ecliptic Pole) by measuring the expansion or retraction of the Obliquity of the Ecliptic, which (angular expanse) of course is identical to the angular distance between the earth's Celestial Pole and the Pole of the Ecliptic.

The Great Cycle of Axis Rotation completes itself in 2,160,000 years – for half of that period, 1,080,000 years, the earth's Celestial Pole is moving *toward* union (angular similarity) with the northern Pole of the Ecliptic and for half that period the opposite is true. Actually I read several years ago that the Ancients used to build monuments, at intervals, at the latitudes that marked the limits of the solstices (a measure of the Obliquity of the Ecliptic) so as to track the migration over thousands of years. Unfortunately I cannot find or remember the book in which I noticed this information so as to offer a quote. But I did come across an article somewhere on the Internet referencing this practice among the Chinese, so one can easily search for the information on the Internet.

The Ancients were able to track the movement of the circumpolar constellations and hence precession by the use of the Cross or Swastika. The Cross/Swastika could have been used to track time by measuring the movement of the circumpolar stars, annually or in the Great Year of precession. The method is quite simple – simply place the Cross/Swastika over a graphic of the circumpolar stars, with the origin of the cross centered at the celestial pole, at set intervals, and measure in degrees the movement of the stars/constellations through the four quadrants of the Cross. The latitude of an observer is equal to the radius of the circumpolar stars being observed from an observer's location i.e. if you are observing from Latitude North 40 Degrees, the axis of the Celestial Pole is likewise 40 degrees above the northern horizon., which in turn indicates the radius of the non-setting circumpolar stars, also called The Circle of Apparition.

So by overlaying or integrating the Cross onto a graphic of the circumpolar stars at regular intervals of their choosing, with the X axis aligned true East to West and the Y axis aligned true South to North, they were able to chart the precessional movement of the stars/constellations around the celestial polar region, by measuring the stars/constellations migration through the four quadrants of the Cross/Swastika. See the graphics on the following Picture Pages that exemplify this process of charting, however with the *Cross centered at the Pole of the Ecliptic,* so as to measure the movement of the earth's Celestial Pole in its precessional circuit around the Pole of the Ecliptic. The time span between each graphic is an Astrological Age of 2,160 years – graphs are approximations, due to my unskilled graphing. We can easily view the changes in the coordinates of the Celestial Pole as it revolves around the Ecliptic Pole in the process of precession. The following graphics show the path of precession with the Ecliptic Pole positioned at the center; **See Book Four**, *The Astrological Foundation Of The Christ Myth* for graphics that depict the entire cycle of precession *with the earth's Celestial Pole at the center.*

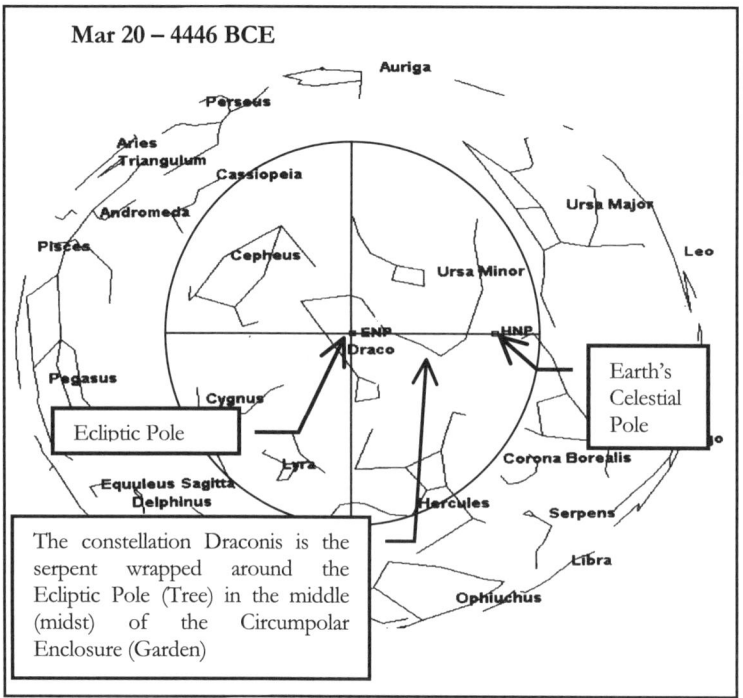

Figure 3: Part one of 4 graphics showing a partial revolution of the Celestial Pole around the Ecliptic Pole in the path of Precession

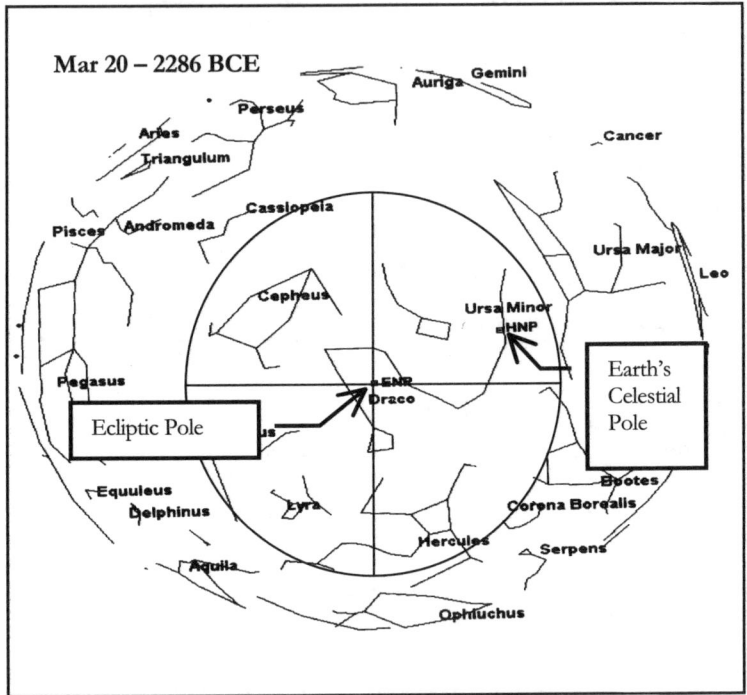

Figure 4: Part 2 of 4 graphs showing revolution of Celestial Pole around the Ecliptic Pole in the path of Precession. Note counterclockwise movement of earth's Pole.

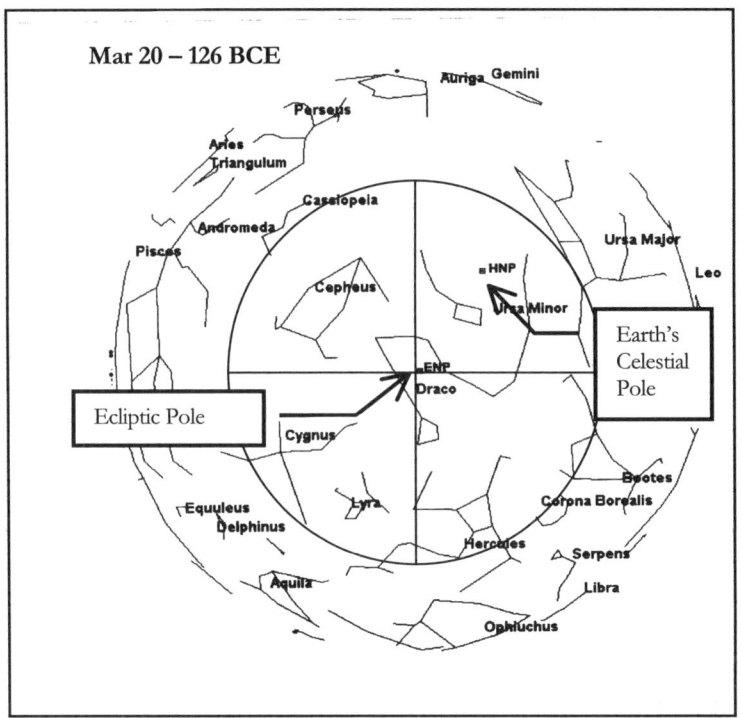

Figure 5: Part 3 of 4 graphs showing revolution of Celestial Pole around the Ecliptic Pole in the path of Precession. Note counterclockwise movement of earth's Pole.

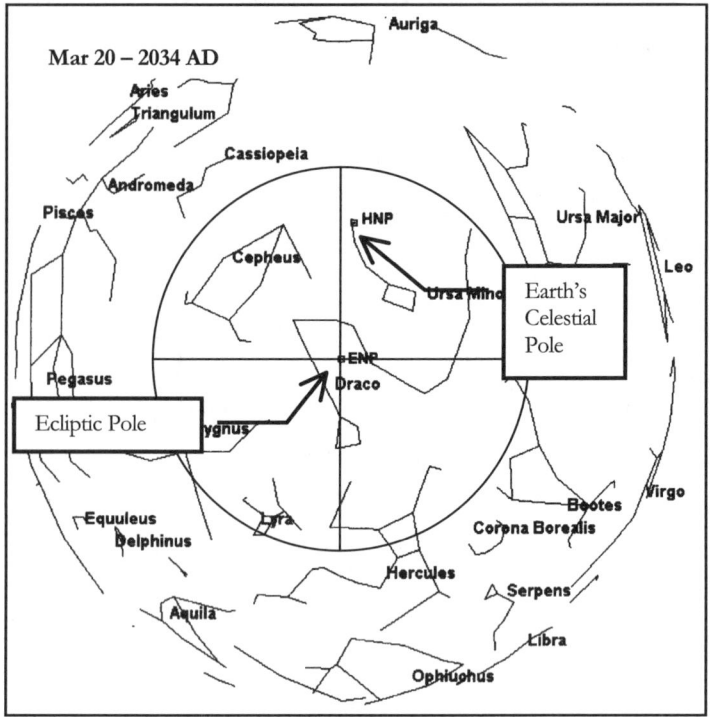

Figure 6: Part 4 of 4 graphics showing the revolution of the Celestial Pole around the Ecliptic Pole in the path of Precession. The 4 graphics cover a time-span of 8,640 year – total Precession cycle is 25,920 years

Astronomers describe precession as a phenomenon caused by the slowly wobbling earth. This definition goes to the probable cause of precession but does not give us a clear concept of how precession appeared to the Ancients. The Ancients saw precession as the revolution of the earth's Celestial Pole around the Pole of the Ecliptic. This correct perception of how the Ancients viewed the path of precession is critical to the proper understanding of the gnosis that was written in reflection of this movement of the two dancing poles, a dance actually imitated by some primitive cultures. You will note that the graph (Figure 2) depicting the path of precession as seen by our astronomers shows the movement of the earth's celestial pole as an ellipse that circles back to its point of origin at the completion of the cycle of 25,920 years; but as noted above, the true course of our Celestial Pole is spiraled.

The Ancients discovered and wrote in their symbolism, graphically and in text that the movement of precession followed the course of a spiral. **They discovered that after the completion of the precessional cycle of 25,920 years the position of the earth's celestial polar axis had actually stepped up four degrees or so in relation to the position of the Pole of the Ecliptic.** This told them that the tilt of the earth's axis was not fixed but rather was rotating or migrating toward angular union with the Pole Of the Ecliptic, at a rate that they calculated and recorded in their symbolism as one degree every 6000 years. This, of course, works out to a cycle of 2,160,000 years for the earth to complete what I have described as the *Great Cycle of Axis Rotation.*

As noted above, the Obliquity of the Ecliptic is what regulates our seasons, and the distribution and duration of sunlight over portions of our planet. Of course, it goes without saying, that our very existence is irrevocably linked to the sun. The sun is not only the creator and sustainer of life, but it is also the destroyer of life on this planet, depending on the intensity and duration of its heat on various sections, and inhabitants of the planet. We must regulate our lives and food production activities in accordance with the cycles of the sun in order to survive. So the Ancients, of necessity, had to closely track the variations in the expanse of the obliquity of the ecliptic for these obvious reasons, pursuant to human survival. But also, far beyond just regulating the seasons, drastic changes in the angular relationships of the ecliptic Pole and the earth's celestial Pole carry implications of climatic and geographical upheavals more devastating and discombobulating than I can find words to describe without engaging into much more research than I have time to complete. These gradual but drastic changes in the obliquity, as we have discussed above, occur regularly over thousands, tens of thousands, hundreds of thousands, and millions of years. The point that I want to emphasize over all others, at this time, is that the Ancients were fixated on the tracking of changes in the obliquity of the ecliptic not only for purposes of gauging the seasons, but also for the more ominous reasons that I have indicated – relating to the gradually shifting Celestial Pole as an indicator of continuous and pronounced, often tragic, environmental transitions over thousands of years.

Cycles of Time

Time is measured by referencing the cycles of celestial entities. We are able to measure the Tropical Year, consisting of 365 days 5 hours 48 minutes 45.51 seconds, by tracking the movement of the sun at its perennial crossing of Cardinal Points. We are able to measure the Sidereal Year, consisting of 365 days 6 hours 9 minutes 9.54 seconds, by tracking the stars annual passing of specific longitudinal coordinates. We are able to measure the Lunar Months by its Phases, the Nodes, the Stars, its alignments with the earth and sun, and Longitude.

The Ancients tracked and measured the seasons and years with great accuracy, initially using somewhat rudimentary methods that nevertheless worked very efficiently. They were able to track the tropical year by monitoring the lengths of the shadows produced by the sun. For residents in the Northern Hemisphere the longest shadow of the year is cast when the sun reaches its lowest declination in the sky at the Winter Solstice. Declination refers to the angular distance of a celestial object above or below the Celestial Equator which marks zero degrees declination – the sun swings between *plus* 23.5 degrees and *minus* 23.5 degrees declination during the course of a year. The low trajectory of the sun at the time of the Winter Solstice, of course, causes the sun's light to cast shadows of objects to longer distances because of the lowered angle of the sun's rays. The reverse occurs at the Summer Solstice when the sun is at its highest declination of the year. Accordingly, by erecting a vertical pole on a leveled surface, and marking the extent of the sun's shadow at high noon each day or at regular intervals, as the sun crossed the meridian, the Ancients were able to record and mark the longest or shortest shadow of the year in correlation to the solstices; thereby measuring one complete year each time the sun's shadow cast by the Pole, or Obelisk, or Pillar touched the designated mark on the pavement. Of course, the Ancients were also able to track the times of the day by similar systems (Sundials) incorporating a gnomon and markings that designated a certain time of the day when touched by the gnomon's shadow.

The Ancients were able to track and measure the Sidereal Year and other cycles by a similar method, again they would erect a Pole as a Front-Site to mark the passing or arrival of a chosen star to a certain coordinate. Of course, in order to aim at a certain position in the night sky, they would also erect a second Pole that served as a Back-Site, thereby creating a straight line aimed at a specific coordinate when viewed from an exact predetermined point of alignment behind the Pole that served as a Back-Site. When the chosen star completed its yearly cycle and returned to alignment with the poles, such would mark the completion of a Sidereal Year. Another method for tracking the stars and other celestial entities was to situate a porthole, small window, or slit in a building so that it aimed toward a particular coordinate, and of course, erect a device (altar for instance) of some type that served as a back-site for the desired trajectory – and when the chosen celestial entity appeared in the opening in line with the back-site, it would mark the passing of whatever cycle that was being gauged. Additionally when incorporating the method of a building (Temple) with a porthole aimed at a specific coordinate which the star, or sun, or moon would pass indicating a cycle of time, they would fashion an insignia (mark, line, mosaic, geometric design, etc.) on the floor or wall so situated i.e. aligned in terms of trajectory with the porthole, as to catch a ray of light to its position from the sun, or moon, or even star, and thereby indicate the completion of a cycle.

Over time, as the Ancients progressed socially, intellectually, and technically, they enhanced their observational techniques. They charted the skies and grouped the stars into constellations; they labeled the stars and constellations with names, royal and common, that mirrored their society, and earthly environment. They learned to measure the horizon, and divided the horizon into 360 degrees with Due North as 0 degrees, Due East as 90 degrees, Due South as 180 degrees, and Due West as 270 degrees. The term Azimuth defines the means by which they measured the horizon. They learned by observation at what degree of azimuth the sun or an observed star would break the horizon on a given date such as the Summer Solstice. The Priests (Astronomers) also learned to calculate points of azimuth at which a star, for instance, would rise above the horizon, with the inclusion of factors that included their Latitude, the declination of the star, and projected date. They built elaborate Observatories by which they would observe the heavenly objects over hundreds and thousands of years, and record their observations – in graphics and literature. Their Observatories were designed to chart the movement of celestial objects on the horizon generally, not on the meridian, as modern astronomers prefer – but they also observed the

Lifting The Gnostic Veil

celestial objects at varying altitudes, as indicated by some Ruins that are still standing.

Temples of the Gods

Their Observatories were not named as such but were called Temples of the Gods. The sun, moon, stars, and planets were often referenced as warriors, gods or demons by the Ancients. In fact they still carry these regal or notorious names today, such as Jupiter, Kronos, Venus, Shamash, Algol, Hermes, and so forth. The Observatories often included many buildings and a wide expanse of land, and were laid out in such a way that they provided ceremonial services for the common people while providing the Priests with astronomically aligned structures by which they could observe and chart the heavens, pursuant to time measurement over hundreds and thousands of years. The common people were not aware of the higher astronomical purposes of these Temple complexes, but rather looked upon them through religious eyes.

For instance, if the Temple was dedicated to the Sun God, that is to say observing or measuring time by the cycles of the sun, the axis of the Temple would be aligned so as to point to the degree of azimuth at which the sun would rise on the date it arrived at the designated Cardinal Point, be it one of the solstices or equinox. If they were measuring the sun cycle as the sun crossed the equinox, then the axis would be laid from west to east, two pillars or a pylon at the eastward entrance to the outer courtyard would serve as a Front-site by which to aim at the point of the sun's rise at the time of the vernal equinox, as the sun rose centered between the pillars on the given date. The Sanctuary of the Sun God, for instance, would serve as the Back-Site, in perfect alignment with the Pillars or center between the Pillars so that the direct rays of the sun would strike directly through the Pillars along the entrance corridor into the Sanctuary at a designated spot where stood an alter, ark, insignia, statue, or whatever representing the Sun-God, the sun's rays so striking and indicating the completion of the Tropical Year. The sanctuaries were always enclosed, covered and dark so that the sun's rays entering the sanctuary would not be diluted or obscured. We all have experienced in the Spring or Fall when the sun crosses the equinox, while driving our cars on some city streets which lay true east and west, that we are blinded by the direct rays of the sun for a few days till the sun passes through those coordinates that mark and are close to zero declination hence due east. This experience is associated with the system by which the Ancients measured the year with precision.

Important reasons why the Ancients were fixated on Timekeeping

I have written this chapter so as to inform my readers of *why* timekeeping was so vitally important to the Ancients, for reasons that go far beyond agriculture and farming. My description for human life on this planet is that it is a Magnificent Predicament. As indicated by this chapter, we, metaphorically, live in the E*ye of the Storm*, a moving seemingly predatory storm, whose fringe winds will certainly decimate and wreak great havoc and destruction on us if we do not continually maneuver so as to *stay* in the Eye Of The Storm where lies relative safety, away from the furor and wrath that surround us, and approaches us over time. It is no wonder that some of the Ancients who were cognizant of the secret Paleo-Gnostic wisdom labeled this life on earth as hell, that Matter is hell. They envisioned that our only path to escape was in the spirit, a *spirit form* that would allow us to return to a previous ethereal state from which we had been banished. Some surmised that this world of torment and potential torment could not be the creation of the true (spiritual) god, but rather is the domain and handiwork of a lesser god – the god of Matter, Satan. They claimed that this life in Matter was the Death Sentence that god promised to Adam and Eve for their disobedience, that captivity of the soul in Matter equates to death. Others added that Jesus Christ had paid the price of death for our parents (Adam and Eve) sins, and now the path to salvation was nigh if we would only have faith. They preached that our salvation lies in escape back to our spiritual father, and that the death of Matter (the body) is actually life, resurrection, or rebirth for the spirit, and the window of escape for the human soul, our immortal spirit – in other words that human life is death (of the spirit) and that human death is rebirth (emancipation of the spirit) pursuant to reunion with the divine. I believe that we have proven, or submitted credible evidences, within the pages of this book that this concept is nothing more than an illusion. We have explained clearly the cosmic and cultural foundations, and references from which this fanciful religious concept, and other similar creeds, was generated. I believe that some people will always prefer the comforting illusions of religious myth, but for we who are incessantly driven by logic - our determined goal is to uncover the veritable truth, a truth that satisfies or at the least pacifies our intellectual hunger for rational explanations of Life, The Universe and the Purpose of it all! – and on this quest, we *must* continue.

Lifting The Gnostic Veil

E p i l o g u e

Truth Verses Illusion

A look at the past and the future

I began this book with the words "this world is an illusion", and indeed I think that we have proven, from the information presented in this book and my other writings, that this assertion is verifiably true. Our world is not what it seems to be. The religious systems of the Ancients followed a two-tier pattern that ran in parallel; each tier or level of interpretation designed to mesh with and nurture the aspirations of the adherents in accordance with their diverse inclinations, desires and hopes. One tier, the *exoteric*, accepted religious doctrine literally, and the other path, the *esoteric*, looked upon religious doctrine as essentially symbolism. For those who sought comforting spiritual explanations for their existence beyond the mundane, and craved solace for their natural fears of death, there was the exoteric level of religion, garnished with utopian fantasies and exalted promises of rewards and life stretching far into boundless eternity – a heaven or paradise reserved for those religious devotees that were pure in heart and unquestioning in their faith. On the other hand, for those of more inquiring and skeptical minds, motivated more by a desire to overcome their doubts, and to verify the dictates of their creeds rationally - and additionally, exhorted by a passion to find the *hidden truth*, there was the avenue of Esotericism or *The Mysteries* as called by some. In reality, a matrix of answers that inevitably led to more questions, and quizzical solutions that engendered new puzzles; but nevertheless an intriguing system that gave sustenance and challenge to those individuals whose rational minds thirsted and craved for logic.

So we have the exoteric path that tends to test and lead us by faith, and the esoteric path that tends to test and lead us by intellect or science, although the science is veiled under layers or *degrees* of mystical symbolism. Whether we follow the path of faith or science, we all, one would think, are desirous of the truth - but this is not so! There are many that would rather avoid the truth because of the emotional burdens or pain associated with it. There are people who will never, ever submit to a truth that runs contrary to their traditional religious beliefs – no matter how many thousands of facts are presented in support of the verifiable truth. This is due, in great part, to the social programming that I alluded to in Chapter One. Another problem is fear, fear of loosing social direction or affiliation - because if one admits or acknowledges that his or her life's cherished traditions are based on lies and/or misconceptions, hence an illusion – where does one go from that point forward – where then lies the meaning and purpose of life? Actually their fears, though understandable, are in fact unwarranted; because in most cases if one has the courage to abandon his or her illusions, one discovers that the illusion was, in fact, a blackened veil, a cloak of darkness that effectively obscured the bright and healing rays of intellectual enlightenment, which when attained, inevitably leads to emotional and spiritual comfort. Be that as it may, historically, the majority, the masses have always favored illusion over truth – just as people generally favor flattery over criticism. Most people prefer being emotionally comfortable, even if that comfort is bought by turning a blind eye to some uncomfortable realities.

Whether doctrinally truthful or not, religion forms a vital and necessary function in society, and has done so as far back as we can detect – in all its multifarious forms. Historically, all societies have produced some form of religious belief. Personally, for what it's worth, my opposition to monotheism is not based on it being false or misleading, which it is in terms of dogma. But - must religion be perfect or divine in order to positively serve and benefit its adherents? I think not - people should have the right to worship god as they see fit (I don't believe that there is a *correct* or *standard* way to worship or serve god) since none of us truly know the identity of the Creator God – we only have our concepts, howbeit some concepts are patently absurd. Nevertheless, religion also provides society with moral and ethical guidelines that are in many ways beneficial and a vital part of our cultural glue. Many argue that we could get such ethical and moral guidance without religion – that may be true, but religion has proved itself to be very efficient in the arena of moral guidance, despite its many, many, many faults.

The problem with monotheism is that it is inherently divisive, as well as intellectually absurd, and incompatible with diverse societies living in peace and brotherhood - *if and when the monotheists take their beliefs seriously.* The driving credo of Jewish, Christian, and Muslim monotheism is that its members are viewed as *the chosen*, special, and elevated in the eyes of god above all others that do not share their beliefs or birthrights. This is doctrinal within monotheism, and although some rank and file members may choose to de-emphasize this aspect of their doctrine – nevertheless it remains that for the fundamentalists and devotees that take their beliefs seriously and literally, this doctrine of religious exclusivity and/or religious elitism is the fuel that nurtures the flames of perpetual strife and contention between diverse cultures. Literal monotheistic doctrine asserts that all humanity must submit to their creeds or be destroyed at Judgment – this amounts to a declaration of war on all those that prefer the right to intellectually choose their faiths or follow the various creeds of their progenitors which may differ with monotheism.

I am sure that monotheism will die a natural death over the coming generations, as we march forth into the Age of Aquarius. A pathway to true international harmony and sincere goodwill will never be securely established so long as significant portions of the earth's population embrace religious beliefs that negate the importance and benefits of reasonable tolerance toward opposing cultural views; and additionally, oppose even the concept of religious and cultural diversity, which (diversity) is irrepressible and inevitable, based on historical precedents.

Lifting The Gnostic Veil

The biggest problem in the world, today, is religion – monotheistic religion specifically. This belief system (monotheism) is the root cause of most of the world's international problems. The pervasive internecine, and international strife that besets us at every turn is basically being fueled by those religious devotees who are attempting to integrate their irrational religious concepts into the politics of a rational world – the two (religion and politics) will never mesh successfully and productively, anymore. **The marriage of religion and government represents the Old World**, which is on its Death Bed, believe it or not – and has been on its Death Bed for centuries, since the dawning of the Age of Reason, The Enlightenment of the 17th century and thereabouts. The mixing of mythologically based religious notions with politics is anathema to intelligent, logical resolutions of social and/or international problems – because religious doctrine is basically irrational. Monotheism is of the **Old World Order**, when Monarchs and Priests pulled the strings of government, and it (monotheism) must eventually terminate, along with the other errors and injustices of the times when Kings and Priests ruled our world. We *need*, must have, and will have a **New Order Of The Ages**, illumined under the Stars of Aquarius, the new Age of Enlightenment, according to some.

We, I believe, are at the brink of a New World System or Age, an Age of Enlightenment, the Age of Aquarius – an Age wherein Reason shall justifiably reign supreme. The signs of Cultural Death are all around us though most of us refuse to acknowledge the signs, be they spiritual or practical. Monotheism has certainly run its course, and will continually diminish, in direct proportion to the elevated intelligence of ensuing generations, who, I suspect, will most certainly not accept being shackled by old superstitions and fallacies. The Age of Enlightenment has been evolving and developing for centuries now, since the intellectual revolts of the 18th century and before when the advancements in science and education ushered some into awareness of the pervasive wiles and deceits

Lifting The Gnostic Veil

of the clergy, and the illegitimacy of the Royalty and Nobility. This enlightenment was witnessed in the American Constitution.

The Founders of this country, and others of that revolutionary era, declared in writing and in deed that America was the birth of a new world (Governmental) system. But what, one may ask, laid at the core of this new system – that the right to govern must be accompanied by the consent of the governed for sure; but beyond that, the prime ingredient of the policy of the new world system was the Separation of Church and State, the nullification of the so-called divine rights of the church (or any religious creed) to interfere religiously in the affairs of government. This was a monumental departure with the policies of the Old World Order. Under the New World System, as proclaimed by those revolutionaries, the influence of the Royalty and their cohorts, along with the Priests and their cohorts over the reins of government was substantially and definitively dismantled; that is to say, the New World System was the successful and decisive realization of the Constitutional Separation of Church and State, and the commencement of a New Order of the Ages (Novus Ordo Seclorum), as evidenced on the Governmental Seal of the United States.

And indeed the founding of this nation was the beginning of a New World System, wherein the powers of the Royalty and the Clergy over governmental policy was broken legislatively, even though the policy or law has not been effectively implemented or enforced as well as one might like to this point in time.

Under the coming Age, society shall be brought to a higher state of spiritual and scientific awareness, I believe, and we shall see the dawning of a *New Faith*; underpinned by concepts based on science and reason, I would suspect following patterns similar to **Deism**, with belief in God as the Great Unknown, and claming no special affiliation with our Creator beyond the gifted spirit of intelligence. I do not believe, as some do, that this New Age will come about by the *conversion* of the masses to a new

Lifting The Gnostic Veil

doctrine – I believe that the Old Concepts shall wither away as the older generations pass away. The effects of culturally based Social Programming are too deep and psychologically binding for most people to effectively counteract. Only a small minority, historically, have shown the wherewithal to radically alter their societal programming under normal political and social environments. In some cases political or economic upheavals may jumpstart the process, when people are *forced to look for other answers* – but true fundamental, and intellectually laced social evolution takes time and generations to confirm. But if the coming generations are properly shielded from the brainwashing tactics of the clergy, and allowed to make informed decisions over time as they come of age, between mythologically based religion and Reason, I have no doubt that they will make the intelligent choice, and in consequence confirm the New Order of the Ages.

History is the window to the future – it is the Crystal Ball through which we can envision things to come. It is a verifiable fact that history repeats itself, that is to say patterns of history repeat throughout the ages. On this basis, we can confidently predict the looming death of monotheism, because such is in accord with the recorded patterns of history. Religions come and go; they sprout up, mature, and eventually wither away – lasting only as long as their formulated doctrines exceed or satisfy the intellect of the general populace, and/or their dogmas are supported and advocated by their political and financial cohorts.

The religions of yesteryear are the historical mythologies of our present era. Most certainly, we study the religions of the ancient Greeks, Persians, Egyptians, Romans, and others – and call those religions of yore *myths*, without a moments regard to how sincerely the Ancients revered their cherished faiths. Our religions of this era will most certainly be the historical mythologies of the coming ages, succumbing to the same fate as our predecessors. There's absolutely no godly or ungodly reason for history to change its patterns.

Epilogue
135

Lifting The Gnostic Veil

History shows further that the religious systems of the Ancients were always dualistic, that is to say, they offered a literal interpretation for the general public, the *exoteric* version; and a more cerebral interpretation for the intellectuals, scholars, priests, the nobility, and others of more discerning intellects, the *esoteric* version. The one version (the exoteric) was designed to bring *spiritual comfort* to the many; and the higher version (the esoteric) was fashioned to bring *intellectual enlightenment* to the few. This ancient theological system has been tested and proved over thousands of years, and shall endure into the indefinite future, in my opinion. Humanity shall, most certainly, over time be brought into higher spiritual awareness, but not necessarily into one accord, or one version of the *truth*. – with all humanity at the same level, or even of the same basic opinion. God is one, but the paths to god are many, according to an old adage.

Lifting The Gnostic Veil

Recommended Readings

1. The Golden Bough, by Sir James George Frazer
2. Star Names Their Lore And Meaning, by Richard Hinckley Allen
3. The Ruins Of Empires, by C. F. Volney
4. Dawn Of Astronomy, by J. Norman Lockyer
5. The Guide For The Perplexed, by Moses Maimonides
6. Morals And Dogma, by Albert Pike
7. Early Christian Doctrines, by J. N. D. Kelly
8. The Worship Of Augustus Caesar, by Alexander Del Mar
9. Earth In Upheaval, by Immanuel Velikovsky
10. Commentaries Of Hierocles On The Golden Verses Of Pythagoras
11. God And The State, by Michael Bakunin
12. Stonehenge Decoded, by Gerald S. Hawkins

Other Books In Print Authored By Malik H Jabbar

1. The Biggest Lie Ever Told, 4th Edition - $9.95

2. The Astrological Foundation Of The Christ Myth - $9.95

3. The Astrological Foundation Of The Christ Myth, Book Two - $14.95

4. The Astrological Foundation Of The Christ Myth, Book Three - $14.95

5. The Astrological Foundation Of The Christ Myth, Book Four - $14.95

Rare Books Distributor

PO Box 13975

Columbus, Ohio 43213

Index

Lifting The Gnostic Veil

Notes

Notes